Google Hacking for Penetration Testers

Third Edition

Google Hacking for Penetration Testers

Third Edition

Johnny Long

Bill Gardner

Justin Brown

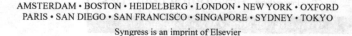

AMSTERDAM • BOSTON • HEIDELBERG • LONDON • NEW YORK • OXFORD
PARIS • SAN DIEGO • SAN FRANCISCO • SINGAPORE • SYDNEY • TOKYO

Syngress is an imprint of Elsevier

Acquiring Editor: Chris Katsaropoulos
Editorial Project Manager: Anna Valutkevich
Project Manager: Punithavathy Govindaradjane
Designer: Matthew Limbert

Syngress is an imprint of Elsevier
225 Wyman Street, Waltham, MA 02451, USA

ISBN: 978-0-12-802964-0

British Library Cataloguing-in-Publication Data
A catalogue record for this book is available from the British Library

Library of Congress Cataloging-in-Publication Data
A catalog record for this book is available from the Library of Congress

For information on all Syngress publications
visit our website at http://store.elsevier.com/Syngress

Working together
to grow libraries in
developing countries

www.elsevier.com • www.bookaid.org

Contents

CHAPTER 1

Google Search Basics

INTRODUCTION

Google's Web interface is unmistakable. It is clean and simple. Its "look and feel" is copyright-protected for good reason. What most people fail to realize is that the interface is also extremely powerful. Throughout this book, we will see how you can use Google to uncover truly amazing things. However, as with most things in life, before you can run, you must learn to walk.

This chapter takes a look at the basics of Google searching. We begin by exploring the powerful Web-based interface that has made Google a household word. Even the most advanced Google users still rely on the Web-based interface for the majority of their day-to-day queries. Once we understand how to navigate and interpret the results from the various interfaces, we will explore basic search techniques.

Understanding basic search techniques will help us build a firm foundation on which to base more advanced queries. You will learn how to properly use the Boolean operators (AND, NOT, and OR), as well as explore the power and flexibility of grouping searches. You will also learn Google's unique implementation of several different wildcard characters. Finally, you will learn the syntax of Google's Uniform Resource Locator (URL) structure.

Learning the ins and outs of the Google URL structure will give you access to greater speed and flexibility when submitting a series of related Google searches. We will see that the Google URL structure provides excellent "shorthand" for exchanging interesting searches with friends and colleagues.

EXPLORING GOOGLE'S WEB-BASED INTERFACE

Google's Web Search Page

The main Google Web page, shown in Figure 1.1, can be found at www.google. com. The interface is known for its clean lines, pleasingly uncluttered presentation and user-friendly layout.

FIGURE 1.1

Although the interface might seem relatively featureless at first glance, we will see that many different search functions can be performed right from the first page.

As shown in Figure 1.1, there's only one place to type. This is the search field. In order to ask Google a question or query, you simply type what you're looking for, then either press Enter (if your browser supports it), or click the Google Search button to be taken to the results page for your query.

Google Web Results Page

After Google processes a search query, it displays a results page. This page lists the results of your search and provides links to the Web pages that contain your search text. The top part of the search result page mimics the main Web search page. Notice the Images, Video, News, Maps, and Gmail links at the top of the page. By clicking these links from a search page, you automatically resubmit your search as another type of search without having to retype your query.

The results line shows which results are displayed (1–10, in this case), the approximate total number of matches (here, over 8 million), the search query itself (including links to dictionary lookups of individual words), and the amount of time the query took to execute.

The speed of the query is often overlooked, but it is quite impressive. Even large queries resulting in millions of hits are returned within a fraction of a second. For each entry on the results page, Google lists the name of the site. This is followed by a summary of the site, usually with the first few lines of content, the URL of the page that matched, the size and date the page was last crawled, a

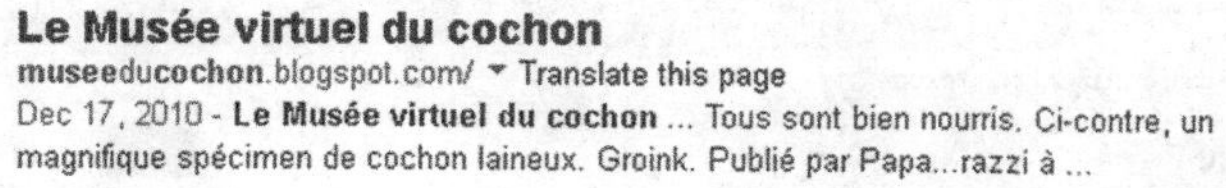

Le Musée virtuel du cochon
museeducochon.blogspot.com/ ▾ Translate this page
Dec 17, 2010 - **Le Musée virtuel du cochon** ... Tous sont bien nourris. Ci-contre, un
magnifique spécimen de cochon laineux. Groink. Publié par Papa...razzi à ...

FIGURE 1.2

cached link that shows the page as it appeared when Google last crawled it, and a link to pages with similar content. If the result page is written in a language other than the default language, and Google supports the translation from that language to the default that is set in the preferences screen, a link titled "Translate this page" will appear, allowing you to read an approximation of that page in your own language (see Figure 1.2).

Google Groups

Due to the surge in popularity of Web-based discussion forums, blogs, mailing lists, and instant messaging technologies, the oldest of public discussion forums, USENET newsgroups, has become an overlooked form of online public discussion. Thousands of users still post to USENET on a daily basis. (A thorough discussion about what USENET encompasses can be found at www.faqs.org/faqs/usenet/what-is/part1/.) DejaNews (www.deja.com) was once considered the authoritative collection point for all past and present newsgroup messages until Google acquired deja.com in February 2001 (see www.google.com/press/pressrel/pressrelease48.html). This acquisition gave users the ability to search the entire archive of USENET messages posted since 1995 via the simple and straightforward Google search interface. Google now refers to USENET groups as Google Groups.

Today, Internet users around the globe turn to Google Groups for general discussion and problem solving. It is very common for Information Technology (IT) practitioners to turn to Google's Groups section for answers to all sorts of technology-related issues. The old USENET community still thrives and flourishes behind the sleek interface of the Google Groups search engine.

The Google Groups search can be accessed by clicking the Groups tab of the main Google Web page, or by surfing to http://groups.google.com. The search interface (shown in Figure 1.3) looks quite different from other Google search pages, yet the search capabilities operate in much the same way. The major difference between the Groups search page and the Web search page lies in the newsgroup browsing links.

Google Image Search

The Google Image search feature allows you to search (at the time of this writing) over a billion graphic files that match your search criteria. Google will attempt to locate your search terms in the image filename, the image caption, the

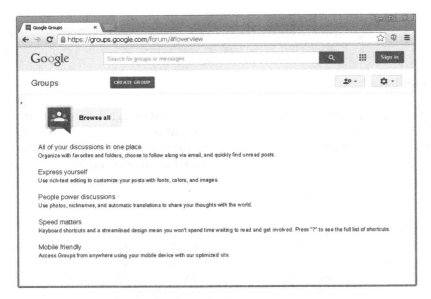

FIGURE 1.3

text surrounding the image, and/or in other undisclosed locations to return a somewhat "de-duplicated" list of images that match your search criteria. The Google Image search operates identically to the Web search with the exception of a few of the advanced search terms, which we will discuss in the next chapter.

The page header looks familiar but contains a few additions unique to the search results page. The Moderate SafeSearch link below the search field allows you to enable or disable images that may be sexually explicit. The Showing dropdown box (located in the Results line) allows you to narrow image results by size. Below the header, each matching image is shown in a thumbnail view with the original resolution and size, followed by the name of the site that hosts the image.

Google Preferences

You can access the Preferences page by clicking the Preferences link from any Google search page or by browsing to www.google.com/preferences. These options primarily pertain to language and locality settings. The Interface Language option describes the language that Google will use when printing tips and informational messages. In addition, this setting controls the language of text printed on Google's navigation items, such as buttons and links. Google assumes that the language you select here is your native language and will "speak" to you in this language whenever possible. Setting this option is not the same as using the translation features of Google (discussed in the following

FIGURE 1.4

section). Web pages written in French will still appear in French, regardless of what you select here.

To get an idea of how Google's Web pages would be altered by a change in the interface language, take a look at Figure 1.4 to see Google's main page rendered in "hacker speak." In addition to changing this setting on the preferences screen, you can access all language specific Google interfaces directly from the Language Tools screen at www.google.com/language_tools.

By default, Google will always try to locate Web pages written in any language. Even though the main Google Web page is now rendered in "hacker speak," Google is still searching for Web pages written in any language. If you are interested in locating Web pages that are written in a particular language, modify the Search Language setting on the Google preferences page.

SafeSearch Filtering blocks explicit sexual content from appearing in Web searches.

Although this is a welcome option from day-to-day Web searching, this option should be disabled when you're performing searches as part of a vulnerability assessment. If sexually explicit content exists on a Web site whose primary content is not sexual in nature, the existence of this material may be of interest to the site owner.

The Number of Results setting describes how many results are displayed on each search result page. This option is highly subjective, based on your tastes and Internet connection speed. However, you may quickly discover that the default setting of 10 hits per page is simply not enough. If you're on a relatively fast connection, you should consider setting this to 100, the maximum number of results per page as shown in Figure 1.5.

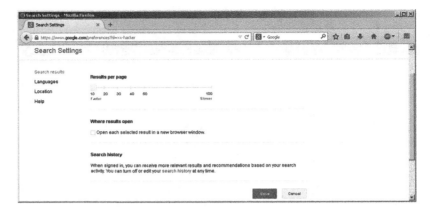

FIGURE 1.5

When checked, the Results Window setting opens search results in a new browser window. This setting is subjective based on your personal tastes. Checking or unchecking this option should have no ill effects unless your browser (or other software) detects the new window as a pop-up advertisement and blocks it. If you notice that your Google results pages are not displaying after you click the Search button, you might want to uncheck this setting in your Google preferences. As noted at the bottom of this page, these changes won't stick unless you have enabled cookies in your browser.

Language Tools

The Language Tools screen, accessed from the main Google page, offers several different utilities for locating and translating Web pages written in different languages. If you rarely search for Web pages written in other languages, it can become cumbersome to modify your preferences before performing this type of search. The first portion of the Language Tools screen allows you to perform a quick search for documents written in other languages, as well as documents located in other countries. The Language Tools screen also includes a utility that performs basic translation services.

The translation form allows you to paste a block of text from the clipboard or supply a Web address to a page that Google will translate into a variety of languages.

In addition to the translation options available from this screen, Google integrates translation options into the search results page. The translation options available from the search results page are based on the language options that are set from the Preferences screen. In other words, if your interface language is set to English, and a Web page listed in a search result is French, Google will

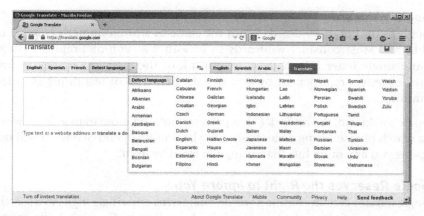

FIGURE 1.6

give you the option to translate that page into language of your preference, English. The list of available language translations is shown in Figure 1.6.

Building Google Queries

Google query building is a process. There's really no such thing as an incorrect search. It's entirely possible to create an ineffective search, but with the explosive growth of the Internet and increasing size of Google's cache, a query that's inefficient today may just provide good results tomorrow – or next month, or next year. The idea behind effective Google searching is to get a firm grasp on the basic syntax and then to get a good grasp of effective narrowing techniques.

Learning the Google query syntax is the easy part. Learning to effectively narrow searches can take some time and requires a bit of practice. Eventually, it will become second nature to find the required information from the plethora of available Web sites.

The Golden Rules of Google Searching

Before we discuss Google searching, we should understand some of the basic ground rules:

Google Queries are not Case Sensitive

Google doesn't care if you type your query in lowercase letters (hackers), uppercase (HACKERS), camel case (hAcKeR), or psycho-case (haCKeR). The word is always regarded the same way. This is especially important when you're searching things such as source code listings, when the case of the term carries a great deal of meaning for the programmer. The one notable exception is the word "or." When used as the Boolean operator, "or" must be written in uppercase as OR.

Google Wildcards

Google's concept of wildcards is not the same as a programmer's concept of wildcards. Most consider wildcards to be either a symbolic representation of any single letter (UNIX users may think of the question mark), or any series of letters represented by an asterisk. This type of technique is called stemming.

Google's wildcard, the asterisk (*), represents nothing more than a single word in a search phrase. Using an asterisk at the beginning or end of a word will not provide you any more hits than using the word by itself.

Google Reserves the Right to Ignore You

Google ignores certain common words, characters, and single digits in a search. These are sometimes called stop words. According to Google's basic search document (www.google.com/help/basics.html), these words include where and how. However, Google does seem to include those words in a search. For example, a search for WHERE 1 = 1 returns less results than a search for 1 = 1. This is an indication that the WHERE is being included in the search. A search for where pig returns significantly less results than a simple search for pig, again an indication that Google does in fact include words like how and where. Sometimes Google will silently ignore these stop words. For example, a search for HOW 1 = WHERE 4 returns the same number of results as a query for 1 = WHERE 4. This seems to indicate that the word HOW is irrelevant to the search results, and that Google silently ignored the word. There are no obvious rules for the word exclusion, but sometimes when Google ignores a search term, a notification will appear on the results page just below the query box.

32-Word Limit

Google limits searches up to 32 words, which is up from the previous limit of 10 words. This includes search terms as well as advanced operators, which we'll discuss in a moment. While this is sufficient for most users, there are ways to get beyond that limit. One way is to replace some terms with the wildcard character (*). Google does not count the wildcard character as a search term, allowing you to extend your searches quite a bit. Consider a query for the wording of the beginning of the US Constitution: "We the people of the United States in order to form a more perfect union establish justice."

This search term is seventeen words long. If we replace some of the words with the asterisk (the wildcard character) and submit it as "we * people * * united states * order * form * more perfect * establish *" including the quote, Google sees this as a nine-word query with eight uncounted wildcard characters. We could extend our search even further by two more real words and just about any number of wildcards.

Basic Searching

Google searching is a process, the goal of which is to find information about a topic. The process begins with a basic search, which is modified in a variety of ways until only the pages of relevant information are returned. Google's ranking technology helps this process along by placing the highest-ranking pages on the first results page. The details of this ranking system are complex and somewhat speculative, but it suffices to say that for our purposes, Google rarely gives us exactly what we need following a single search.

The simplest Google query consists of a single word or a combination of individual words typed into the search interface. Some basic word searches could include:

- hacker
- FBI hacker Mitnick
- mad hacker dpak

Slightly more complex than a word search is a phrase search. A phrase is a group of words enclosed in double-quote marks. When Google encounters a phrase, it searches for all words in that phrase in the exact order you provide them. Google does not exclude common words found in a phrase. Phrase searches can include:

- "Google hacker"
- "adult humor"
- "Carolina gets pwnt"

Phrase and word searches can be combined and used with advanced operators, as we will see in the next chapter.

Using Boolean Operators and Special Characters

More advanced than basic word searches, phrase searches are still a basic form of a Google query. To perform advanced queries, it is necessary to understand the Boolean operators AND, OR, and NOT. To properly segment the various parts of an advanced Google query, we must also explore visual grouping techniques that use the parenthesis characters. Finally, we will combine these techniques with certain special characters that may serve as shorthand for certain operators, wildcard characters, or placeholders.

If you have used any other Web search engines, you have probably been exposed to Boolean operators. Boolean operators help specify the results that are returned from a query. If you are already familiar with Boolean operators, take a moment to skim this section to help you understand Google's particular implementation of these operators, since many search engines handle them in different ways. Improper use of these operators could drastically alter the results that are returned.

The most commonly used Boolean operator is AND. This operator is used to include multiple terms in a query. For example, a simple query like hacker could be expanded with a Boolean operator by querying for hacker AND cracker. The latter query would include not only pages that talk about hackers, but also sites that talk about hackers and the snacks they might eat. Some search engines require the use of this operator, but Google does not. The term AND is redundant to Google. By default, Google automatically searches for all the terms you include in your query. In fact, Google will warn you when you have included terms that are obviously redundant.

The plus symbol (+) forces the inclusion of the word that follows it. There should be no space following the plus symbol. For example, if you were to search for "and," "justice," "for," and "all" as separate, distinct words, Google would warn that several of the words are too common and are excluded from the search. To force Google to search for those common words, preface them with the plus sign. It's okay to go overboard with the plus sign. It has no ill effects if it is used excessively. To perform this search with the inclusion of all words, consider a query such as +and justice for +all. In addition, the words could be enclosed in double quotes. This generally will force Google to include all the common words in the phrase. This query presented as a phrase would be: "and justice for all."

Another common Boolean operator is NOT. Functionally the opposite of the AND operator, the NOT operator excludes a word from a search. The best way to use this operator is to preface a search word with the minus sign (−). Be sure to leave no space between the minus sign and the search term. Consider a simple query, such as hacker. This query is very generic and will return hits for all sorts of occupations like golfers, woodchoppers, serial killers, and those with chronic bronchitis. With this type of query, you are most likely not interested in each and every form of the word hacker but rather a more specific rendition of the term. To narrow the search, you could include more terms, which Google would automatically AND together, or you could start narrowing the search by using NOT to remove certain terms from your search. To remove some of the more unsavory characters from your search, consider using queries such as hacker −golf or hacker −phlegm. This would allow you to get closer to the dastardly wood choppers you're looking for. Or, you could try a Google Video search for lumberjack song. Talk about twisted.

A less common and sometimes more confusing Boolean operator is OR. The OR operator, represented by the pipe symbol (|) or simply the word OR in uppercase letters, instructs Google to locate either one term or another in a query. Although this seems fairly straightforward when considering a simple query, such as "evil cybercriminal" or hacker, things can get terribly confusing when you string together a bunch of ANDs, ORs and NOTs. To help alleviate this confusion, don't think of the query as anything more than a sentence read from left to right. Forget all that order of operations stuff you learned in high school algebra. For our purposes, an AND is weighed equally with an OR, which is weighed as equally as an advanced operator. These factors may affect the rank or order in which the search results appear on the page, but have no bearing on how Google handles the search query.

Let's take a look at a very complex example, the exact mechanics of which we will discuss in Chapter 2: intext:password | passcode intext:username | userid | user filetype:csv. This example uses advanced operators combined with the OR Boolean to create a query that reads like a sentence written as a polite request. The request reads, "Locate all pages that have either password or passcode in the text of the document. From those pages, show me only the pages that contain either the words username, userid, or user in the text of the document. From those pages, only show me documents that are CSV files." Google doesn't get confused by the fact that technically those OR symbols break up the query into all sorts of possible interpretations. Google isn't bothered by the fact that from an algebraic standpoint, your query is syntactically wrong. For the purposes of learning how to create queries, all we need to remember is that Google reads our query from left to right.

Google's cut-and-dried approach to combining Boolean operators is still very confusing to the reader. Fortunately, Google is not offended (or affected by) parenthesis. The previous query can also be submitted as intext:(password | passcode) intext:(username | userid | user) filetype:csv. This query is infinitely more readable for us humans, and it produces exactly the same results as the more confusing query that lacked parentheses.

Search Reduction

To achieve the most relevant results, you'll often need to narrow your search by modifying the search query. Although Google tends to provide very relevant results for most basic searches, we will begin looking at fairly complex searches aimed at locating a very narrow subset of Web sites. The vast majority of this book focuses on search reduction techniques and suggestions, but it's important that you at least understand the basics of search reduction.

As a simple example, we'll take a look at GNU Zebra, free software that manages Transmission Control Protocol (TCP)/Internet Protocol (IP)-based routing protocols. GNU Zebra uses a file called zebra.conf to store configuration settings, including interface information and passwords. After downloading the latest version of Zebra from the Web, we learn that the included zebra.conf. sample file looks like this:

```
! -*- zebra -*-

!

! zebra sample configuration file

!

! $Id: zebra.conf.sample,v 1.14 1999/02/19 17:26:38 developer Exp $

!

hostname Router

password zebra

enable password zebra

!

! Interface's description.

!

!interface lo

! description test ofdesc.

!

!interface sit0

! multicast

!

! Static default route sample.

!

!ip route 0.0.0.0/0 203.181.89.241

!

!log file zebra.log
```

To attempt to locate these files with Google, we might try a simple search such as:

"! Interface's description." This is considered the base search. Base searches should be as unique as possible in order to get as close to our desired results as possible, remembering the old adage, "Garbage in, garbage out." Starting with a poor base search completely negates all the hard work you'll put into reduction. Our base search is unique not only because we have focused on

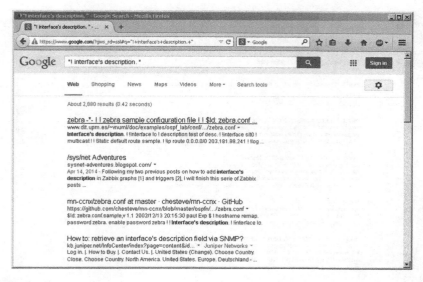

FIGURE 1.7

the words Interface's and description, but we have also included the exclamation mark, the spaces, and the period following the phrase as part of our search. This is the exact syntax that the configuration file itself uses, so this seems like a very good place to start. However, Google takes some liberties with this search query, making the results less than adequate, as shown in Figure 1.7. looking for zebra.conf files. So let's add this to our search to help narrow the results. This makes our next query: "! Interface's description." zebra.conf.

As Figure 1.8 shows, the results are slightly different but not necessarily better.

For starters, the SeattleWireless hit we had in our first search is missing. This was a valid hit, but because the configuration file was not named zebra.conf, (it was named ZebraConfig) our "improved" search doesn't see it. This is a great lesson to learn about search reduction: don't reduce your way past valid results.

These sample files may clutter valid results, so we'll add to our existing query, reducing hits that contain this phrase. This makes our new query: "! Interface's description." – "zebra.conf.sample".

Now, it helps to step into the shoes of the software's users for just a moment. Software installations like this one often ship with a sample configuration file to help guide the process of setting up a custom configuration. Most users will simply edit this file, changing only the settings that need to be changed for their environments, saving the file not as a .sample file but as a .conf file.

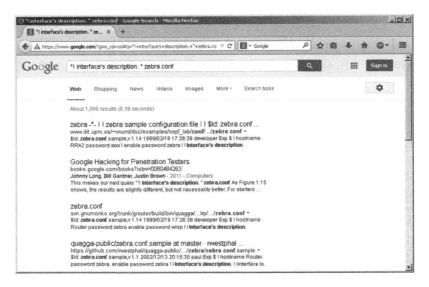

FIGURE 1.8

In this situation, the user could have a live configuration file with the term zebra.conf.sample still in place. Reduction based on this term may remove valid configuration files created in this manner.

There's yet another reduction angle. Notice that our zebra.conf.sample file contained the term hostname Router. This is most likely one of the settings that a user will change; although we're making an assumption that his machine is not named Router. This is less a gamble than reducing based on zebra.conf. sample, however. Adding the reduction term "hostname Router" to our query brings our results number down and reduces our hits on potential sample files, all without sacrificing potential live hits.

Although it's certainly possible to keep reducing, often it's enough to make just a few minor reductions that can be validated by eye than to spend too much time coming up with the perfect search reduction. Our final (that's four qualifiers for just one word!) query becomes: "! Interface's description." – "hostname Router". This is not the best query for locating these files, but it's good enough to give you an idea about how search reduction works. As we'll see in Chapter 2, advanced operators will get us even closer to that perfect query.

Working With Google URLs

Advanced Google users begin testing advanced queries right from the Web interface's search field, refining queries until they are just right. Every Google query can be represented with a URL that points to the results page. Google's results pages are not static pages. They are dynamic and are created on the fly when you click the Search button or activate a URL that links to a results page. Submitting a search through the Web interface takes you to a results page that can be represented by a single URL. For example, consider the query ihackstuff. Once you enter this query, you are whisked away to a URL similar to the following: www.google.com/search?q=ihackstuff. If you bookmark this URL and return to it later, or simply enter the URL into your browser's address bar, Google will reprocess your search for ihackstuff and display the results.

This URL then becomes not only an active connection to a list of results, but it also serves as a nice, compact sort of shorthand for a Google query. Any experienced Google searcher can take a look at this URL and realize the search subject. This URL can also be modified fairly easily. By changing the word ihackstuff to iwritestuff, the Google query is changed to find the term iwritestuff. This simple example illustrates the usefulness of the Google URL for advanced searching. A quick modification of the URL can make changes happen fast!

URL Syntax

To fully understand the power of the URL, we need to understand the syntax. The first part of the URL, www.google.com/search, is the location of Google's search script. I refer to this URL, as well as the question mark that follows it, as the base or starting URL. Browsing to this URL presents you with a nice, blank search page. The question mark after the word search indicates that parameters are about to be passed into the search script. Parameters are options that instruct the search script to actually do something. Parameters are separated by the ampersand (&) and consist of a variable followed by the equal sign (=), followed by the value that the variable should be set to. The basic syntax will look something like this: www.google.com/search?variable1=value&variable 2=value. This URL contains very simple characters. More complex URL's will contain special characters, which must be represented with hex code equivalents. Let's take a second to talk about hex encoding.

Special Characters

Hex encoding is definitely geek stuff, but sooner or later you may need to include a special character in your search URL. When that time comes, it's best to just let your browser help you out. Most modern browsers will adjust a typed URL, replacing special characters and spaces with hex-encoded equivalents. If your browser supports this behavior, your job of URL construction is that much easier. Try this simple test: Type the following URL in your browser's address bar, making sure to use spaces between i, hack, and stuff: www.google.com/search?q="i hack stuff". If your browser supports this autocorrecting feature, after you press Enter in the address bar, the URL should be corrected to www.google.com/search?q="i%20hack%20stuff", or something similar. Notice that the spaces were changed to %20. The percent sign indicates that the next two digits are the hexadecimal value of the space character, 20. Some browsers will take the conversion one step further, changing the double-quotes to %22 as well. If your browser refuses to convert those spaces, the query will not work as expected. There may be a setting in your browser to modify this behavior. If not, do yourself a favor and use a modern browser. Internet Explorer, Firefox, Safari, Chrome, and Opera are all excellent choices.

Putting the Pieces Together

Google search URL construction is like putting together Legos. You start with a URL, and you modify it as needed to achieve varying search results. Many times your base URL will come from a search you submitted, via the Google Web interface. If you need some added parameters, you can add them directly to the base URL in any order. If you need to modify parameters in your search, you can change the value of the parameter and resubmit your search. If you need to remove a parameter, you can delete that entire parameter from the URL and re-submit your search. This process is especially easy if you are modifying the URL directly in your browser's address bar. You simply make changes to the URL and press Enter. The browser will automatically fetch the address and take you to an updated search page. You could achieve similar results by poking around Google's advanced search page (www.google.com/advanced_search, shown in Figure 1.9), and by setting various preferences, as discussed earlier. Ultimately, most advanced users find it faster and easier to make quick search adjustments directly through URL modification.

A Google search URL can contain many different parameters. Depending on the options you selected and the search terms you provided, you will see some

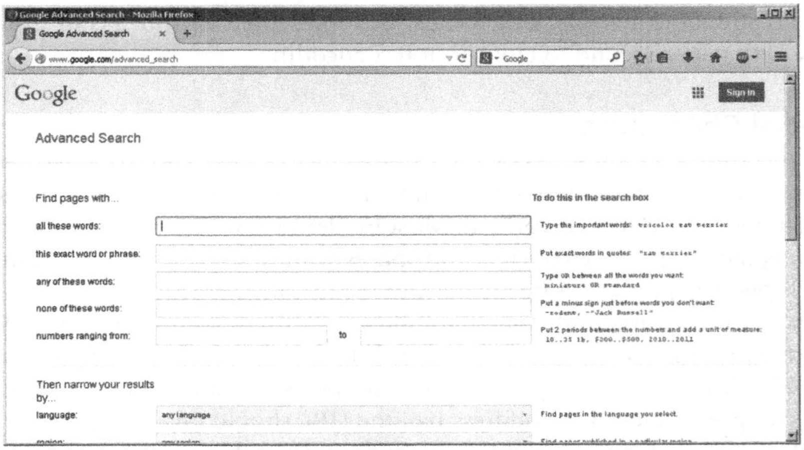

FIGURE 1.9

FIGURE 1.10

or all of the variables listed. These parameters can be added or modified as needed to change your search criteria. Some parameters accept a language restrict (lr) code as a value. The lr value instructs Google to only return pages written in a specific language. For example, lr = lang_ar only returns pages written in Arabic. The hl variable changes the language of Google's messages and links. This is not the same as the lr variable, which restricts our results to pages written in a specific language, nor is it like the translation service, which translates a page from one language to another.

To understand the contrast between hl and lr, consider the food search resubmitted as an lr search, as shown in Figure 1.10. Notice that our URL is different: There are now far fewer results. The search results are written in Danish, Google added a Search Danish pages button, and Google's messages and links are written in English. Unlike the hl option, the lr option changes our search results. We have asked Google to return only pages written in Danish.

The restrict variable is easily confused with the lr variable, since it restricts your search to a particular language. However, restrict has nothing to do with language. This variable gives you the ability to restrict your search results to one or more countries, determined by the top-level domain name (.us, for example), and/or by geographic location of the server's IP address. If you think this seems somewhat inexact, you're right. Although inexact, this variable works amazingly well. Consider a search for people, in which we restrict our results to JP (Japan), as shown in Figure 1.11. Our URL has changed to include the restrict value but notice that the second hit is from www.unu.edu, the location of which is unknown. As our sidebar reveals, the host does in fact appear to be located in Japan.

SUMMARY

Google is deceptively simple in appearance, but offers many powerful options that provide the groundwork for powerful searches. Many different types of content can be searched, including Web pages, message groups such as USENET,

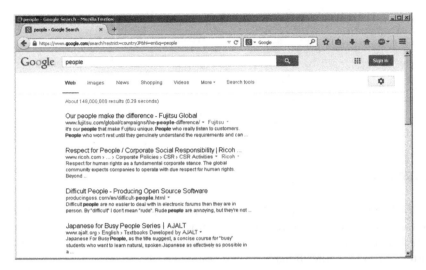

FIGURE 1.11

images, video, and more. Beginners to Google searching are encouraged to use the Google-provided forms for searching, paying close attention to the messages and warnings Google provides about syntax. Boolean operators, such as OR and NOT, are available through the use of the minus sign and the word OR (or the | symbol) respectively, whereas the AND operator is ignored, since Google automatically includes all terms in a search. Advanced search options are available through the Advanced Search page, which allows users to narrow search results quickly. Advanced Google users narrow their searches through customized queries and a healthy dose of experience and good old common sense.

FAST TRACK SOLUTIONS

Exploring Google's Web-Based Interface

There are several distinct Google search areas (including Web, group, video, and image searches), each with distinct searching characteristics and results pages.

The Web search page, the heart and soul of Google, is simple, streamlined, and powerful, enabling even the most advanced searches.

A Google Groups search allows you to search all past and present newsgroup posts.

The Image search feature allows you to search for nearly a billion graphics by keyword.

Google's preferences and language tools enable search customization, translation services, language-specific searches, and much more.

Building Google Queries

Google query building is a process that includes determining a solid base search and expanding or reducing that search to achieve the desired results. Always remember the golden rules of Google searching. These basic premises serve as the foundation for a successful search.

Used properly, Boolean operators and special characters help expand or reduce searches. They can also help clarify a search for fellow humans who might read your queries later on.

Working With Google URLs

Once a Google query has been submitted, you are whisked away to the Google results page, the URL of which can be used to modify a search or recall it later.

Although there are many different variables that can be set in a Google search URL, the only one that is really required is the q, or query, variable. Some advanced search options, such as as_qdr (date-restricted search by month), cannot be easily set anywhere besides the URL.

Links to Sites

www.google.com: This is the main Google Web page, the entry point for most searches.

http://groups.google.com: The Google Groups Web page.

http://images.google.com: Search Google for images and graphics.

http://video.google.com: Search Google for video files.

www.google.com/language_tools: Various language and translation options.

www.google.com/advanced_search: The advanced search form.

www.google.com/preferences: The Preferences page, which allows you to set options such as interface language, search language, SafeSearch filtering, and number of results per page.

Q: Some people like using nifty toolbars. Where can I find information about Google toolbars?

A: Ask Google. Seriously, if you aren't already in the habit of simply asking Google when you have a Google-related question, you should get in that habit. Google can almost always provide an answer if you can figure out the query.

Here's a list of some popular Google search tools:

Platform Tool Location

Mac Google Notifier, Google; www.google.com/mac.html
Desktop, Google Sketchup PC Google Pack (includes IE and www.google.com/tools Firefox toolbars, Google Desktop and more)

Mozilla Browser Googlebar; http://googlebar.mozdev.org/
Firefox, Internet Groowe multiengine Toolbar; www.groowe.com/
Explorer

Q: Are there any techniques I can use to learn how to build Google URL's?
A: Yes. There are a few ways. First, submit basic queries through the Web
interface and look at the URL that's generated when you submit the search.
From the search results page, modify the query slightly and look at how the
URL changes when you submit it. This boils down to "do it, watch what it does
then do it again." The second way involves using "query builder" programs that
present a graphical interface, which allows you to select the search options
you want, building a Google URL as you navigate through the interface. Keep
an eye on the search engine hacking forums at http://johnny.ihackstuff.com,
specifically the "coders corner" where users discuss programs that perform
this type of functionality.

Frequently Asked Questions

The following frequently asked questions, answered by the authors of this book,
are designed to both measure your understanding of the concepts presented in
this chapter and to assist you with real-life implementation of these concepts.
To have your questions about this chapter answered by the author, browse to
www.syngress.com/solutions and click on the "Ask the Author" form.

Q: What's better? Using Google's interface, using toolbars, or writing URL's?
A: It's not fair to claim that any one technique is better than the others. It boils
down to personal preference, and many advanced Google users use each of
these techniques in different ways. Many lengthy Google sessions begin as a
simple query typed into the www.google.com Web interface. Depending on the
narrowing process, it may be easier to add or subtract from the query right
in the search field. Other times, like in the case of the date range operator
(covered in Chapter 2), it may be easier to add a quick as_qdr parameter to the
end of the URL. Toolbars excel at providing you quick access to a Google search
while you're browsing another page. Most toolbars allow you to select text on a
page, right-click on the page and select "Google search" to submit the selected
text as a query to Google. Which technique you decide to use ultimately
depends on your tastes and the context in which you perform searches.

CHAPTER 2

Advanced Operators

INTRODUCTION

Beyond the basic searching techniques explored in the previous chapter, Google offers special terms known as advanced operators to help you perform more advanced queries. These operators, used properly, can help you get to exactly the information you're looking for without spending too much time poring over page after page of search results. When advanced operators are not provided in a query, Google will locate your search terms in *any* area of the Web page, including the title, the text, the Uniform Resource Locator (URL), or the like. We will take a look at the following advanced operators in this chapter:

- intitle, allintitle
- inurl, allinurl
- filetype
- allintext
- site
- link
- inanchor
- daterange
- cache
- info
- related
- phonebook
- rphonebook
- bphonebook
- author
- group
- msgid
- insubject
- stocks
- define

OPERATOR SYNTAX

Advanced operators are additions to a query designed to narrow down the search results. Although they are relatively easy to use, they have a fairly rigid syntax that must be followed. The basic syntax of an advanced operator is *operator:search_term*. When using advanced operators, keep in mind the following:

- There is no space between the operator, the colon, and the search term. Violating this syntax can produce undesired results and will keep Google from understanding what you are trying to do. In most cases, Google will treat a syntactically bad advanced operator as just another search term. For example, providing the advanced operator *intitle* without a following colon and search term will cause Google to return pages that contain the word *intitle*.
- The *search_term* portion of an operator search follows the syntax discussed in the previous chapter. For example, a search term can be a single word or a phrase surrounded by quotes. If you use a phrase, just make sure there are no spaces between the operator, the colon, and the first quote of the phrase.
- Boolean operators and special characters (such as *OR* and +) can still be applied to advanced operator queries, but be sure they don't get in the way of the separating colon.
- Advanced operators can be combined in a single query as long as you honor both the basic Google query syntax as well as the advanced operator syntax. Some advanced operators combine better than others, and some simply cannot be combined. We will take a look at these limitations later in this chapter.
- The *ALL* operators (the operators beginning with the word *ALL*) are oddballs. They are generally used once per query and cannot be mixed with other operators.

Examples of valid queries that use advanced operators include these:

- *intitle:Google* – This query will return pages that have the word *Google* in their title.
- *intitle:"index of"* – This query will return pages that have the phrase *"index of"* in their title. Remember from the previous chapter that this query could also be given as *"intitle:index.of"*, since the period serves as any character. This technique also makes it easy to supply a phrase without having to type the spaces and the quotation marks around the phrase.
- *intitle:"index of" private* – This query will return pages that have the phrase *"index of"* in their title and also have the word *"private"* anywhere in the page, including in the URL, the title, the text, and so on. Notice

that *"intitle"* only applies to the phrase *"index of"* and not the word *"private,"* since the first unquoted space follows the phrase *"index of."* Google interprets that space as the end of your advanced operator search term and continues processing the rest of the query.

- *intitle:"index of" "backup files"* – This query will return pages that have the phrase "index of" in their title and the phrase *"backup files"* anywhere in the page, including the URL, the title, the text, and so on. Again, notice that *"intitle"* only applies to the phrase *"index of."*

TROUBLESHOOTING YOUR SYNTAX

Before we jump head first into the advanced operators, let's talk about trouble-shooting the inevitable syntax errors you'll run into when using these operators. Google is kind enough to tell you when you've made a mistake, as shown in Figure 2.1.

In this example, we tried to give Google an invalid option to the *as_qdr* variable in the URL. (The correct syntax would be *as_qdr = m3*, as we'll see later.) Google's search result page listed right at the top that there was some sort of problem. These messages are often the key to unraveling errors in either your query string or your URL, so keep an eye on the top of the results page. We've found that it's easy to overlook this spot on the results page, since we normally scroll past it to get down to the results.

Sometimes, however, Google is less helpful, returning a blank results page with no error text, as shown in Figure 2.2.

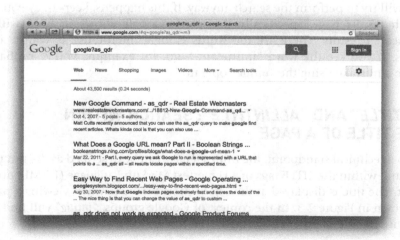

FIGURE 2.1

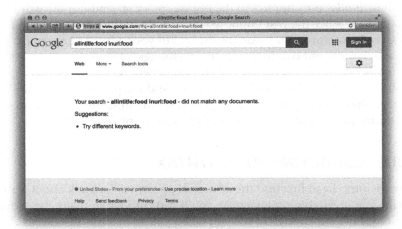

FIGURE 2.2

INTRODUCING GOOGLE'S ADVANCED OPERATORS

Google's advanced operators are very versatile, but not all operators can be used everywhere, as we saw in the previous example. Some operators can only be used in performing a Web search, and others can only be used in a Groups search. If you have trouble remembering these rules, keep an eye on the results line near the top of the page. If Google picks up on your bad syntax, an error message will be displayed, letting you know what you did wrong. Sometimes, however, Google will not pick up on your bad form and will try to perform the search anyway. If this happens, keep an eye on the search results page, specifically the words Google shows in bold within the search results. These are the words Google interpreted as your search terms. If you see the word "intitle" in bold, for example, you've probably made a mistake using the *"intitle"* operator.

"INTITLE" AND *"ALLINTITLE"*: SEARCH WITHIN THE TITLE OF A PAGE

From a technical standpoint, the title of a page can be described as the text that is found within the TITLE tags of a Hypertext Markup Language (HTML) document. The title is displayed at the top of most browsers when viewing a page, as shown in Figure 2.3. In the context of Google groups, *"intitle"* will find the term in the title of the message post.

FIGURE 2.3

As shown in Figure 2.3, the title of the Web page is *"Syngress Publishing."* It is important to realize that some Web browsers will insert text into the title of a Web page, under certain circumstances.

This time, the title of the page is prepended with the word "Loading" and quotation marks, which were inserted by the Safari browser. When using *intitle*, be sure to consider what text is actually from the title and which text might have been inserted by the browser.

Title text is not limited, however, to the *TITLE HTML* tag. A Web page's document can be generated in any number of ways, and in some cases, a Web page might not even have a title at all. The thing to remember is that the title is the text that appears at the top of the Web page, and you can use *"intitle"* to locate text in that spot.

When using *"intitle"*, it's important that you pay special attention to the syntax of the search string, since the word or phrase following the word *"intitle"* is considered the search phrase. *"Allintitle"* breaks this rule. *"Allintitle"* tells Google that every single word or phrase that follows is to be found in the title of the page. For example, we just looked at the *intitle:"index of""backup files"* query as an example of an *"intitle"* search. In this query, the term "backup files" is found not in the title of the second hit but rather in the text of the document, as shown in Figure 2.4.

If we were to modify this query to *allintitle:"index of""backup files"* we would get a different response from Google, as shown in Figure 2.5.

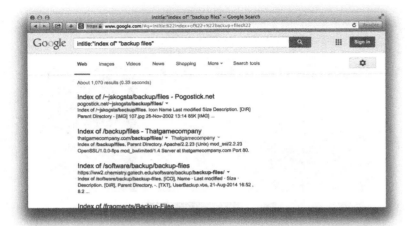

FIGURE 2.4

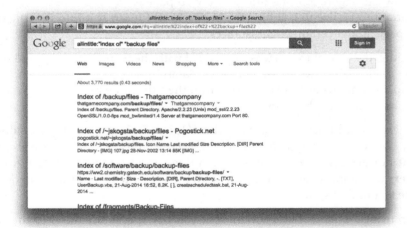

FIGURE 2.5

Now, every hit contains both *"index of"* and *"backup files"* in the title of each hit. Notice also that the *"allintitle"* search is also more restrictive, returning only a fraction of the results as the *"intitle"* search.

Be wary of using the *"allintitle"* operator. It tends to be clumsy when it's used with other advanced operators and tends to break the query entirely, causing it to return no results. It's better to go overboard and use a bunch of *"intitle"* operators in a query rather than using *"allintitle operators."*

ALLINTEXT: LOCATE A STRING WITHIN THE TEXT OF A PAGE

The *allintext* operator is perhaps the simplest operator to use since it performs the function that search engines are most known for: locating a term within the text of the page. Although this advanced operator might seem too generic to be of any real use, it is handy when you *know* that the text you're looking for should *only* be found in the text of the page. Using *allintext* can also serve as a type of shorthand for "find this string anywhere *except* in the title, the URL, and links." Since this operator starts with the word *all*, every search term provided after the operator is considered part of the operator's search query.

For this reason, the *allintext* operator should not be mixed with other advanced operators.

INURL AND *ALLINURL*: FINDING TEXT IN A URL

Having been exposed to the *intitle* operators, it might seem like a fairly simple task to start throwing around the *inurl* operator with reckless abandon. I encourage such flights of fancy in searching, but first realize that a URL is a much more complicated beast than a simple page title, and the workings of the *inurl* operator can be equally complex.

First, let's talk about what a URL is. Short for Uniform Resource Locator, a URL is simply the address of a Web page. The beginning of a URL consists of a protocol, followed by ://, like the very common *http://* or *ftp://*. Following the protocol is an address followed by a pathname, all separated by forward slashes (/). Following the pathname comes an optional filename. A common basic URL, like http://www.uriah.com/apple-qt/1984.html, can be seen as several different components. The protocol, *http*, indicates that this is basically a Web server. The server is located at www.uriah.com, and the requested file, 1984.html, is found in the /apple-qt directory on the server. As we saw in the previous chapter, a Google search can be conveyed as a URL, which can look something like http://www.google.com/search?q=ihackstuff.

We've discussed the protocol, server, directory, and file pieces of the URL, but that last part of our example URL, *?q = ihackstuff*, bears a bit more examination. Explained simply, this is a list of parameters that are being passed into the "search" program or file. Without going into much more detail, simply understand that all this "stuff" is considered to be part of the URL, which Google can be instructed to search with the *inurl* and *allinurl* operators.

So far this doesn't seem much more complex than dealing with the *intitle* operator, but there are a few complications. First, Google can't effectively search

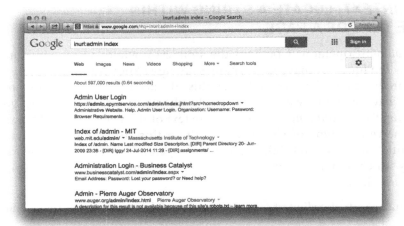

FIGURE 2.6

the protocol portion of the URL – *http://*, for example. Second, there are a ton of special characters sprinkled around the URL, which Google also has trouble weeding through. Attempting to specifically include these special characters in a search could cause unexpected results and might limit your search in un-desired ways. Third, and most important, other advanced operators (*site* and *filetype*, for example) can search more specific places *inside* the URL even better than *inurl* can. These factors make *inurl* much trickier to use effectively than an *intitle* search, which is very simple by comparison. Regardless, *inurl* is one of the most indispensable operators for advanced Google users; we'll see it used extensively throughout this book.

As with the *intitle* operator, *inurl* has a companion operator, known as *allinurl*. Consider the *inurl* search results page shown in Figure 2.6.

This search located the word *admin* in the URL of the document and the word *index* anywhere in the document, returning more than two million results. Re-placing the *intitle* search with an *allintitle* search, we receive the results page shown in Figure 2.7.

This time, Google was instructed to find the words *admin* and *index* only in the URL of the document, resulting in about a million less hits. Just like the *allin-title* search, *allinurl* tells Google that every single word or phrase that follows is to be found only in the URL of the page. And just like *allintitle*, *allinurl* does not play very well with other queries. If you need to find several words or phrases in a URL, it's better to supply several *inurl* queries than to succumb to the rather unfriendly *allinurl* conventions.

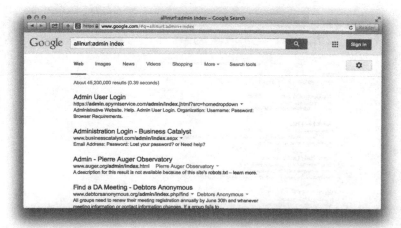

FIGURE 2.7

SITE: NARROW SEARCH TO SPECIFIC SITES

Although technically a part of a URL, the best way to search address (or domain name) of a server is with the *site* operator. *Site* allows you to search only for pages that are hosted on a specific server or in a specific domain. Although fairly straightforward, proper use of the site operator can take a little bit of getting used to, since Google reads Web server names from right to left, as opposed to the human convention of reading site names from left to right. Consider a common Web server name, www.apple.com. To locate pages that are hosted on blackhat. com, a simple query of *site:blackhat.com* will suffice, as shown in Figure 2.8.

Notice that the first two results are from www.blackhat.com and japan. blackhat.com. Both of these servers end in *blackhat.com* and are valid results of our query.

Like many of Google's advanced operators, site can be used in interesting ways. Take, for example, a query for *site:r*, the results of which are shown in Figure 2.9.

Look very closely at the results of the query and you'll discover that the URL for the first returned result looks a bit odd. Truth be told, this result *is* odd. Google (and the Internet at large) reads server names (really *domain names*) from right to left, not from left to right. So a Google query for *site:r* can never return valid results because there is no *.r* domain name. So why does Google return results? It's hard to be certain, but one thing's for sure: these oddball searches and their associated responses are very interesting to advanced search engine users and fuel the fire for further exploration.

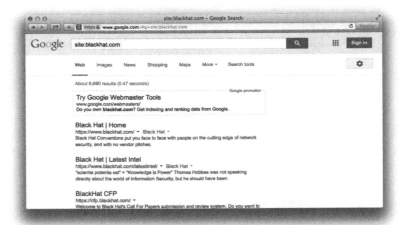

FIGURE 2.8

FIGURE 2.9

The *site* operator can be easily combined with other searches and operators, as we'll see later in this chapter.

FILETYPE: SEARCH FOR FILES OF A SPECIFIC TYPE

Google searches more than just Web pages. Google can search many different types of files, including PDF (Adobe Portable Document Format) and Microsoft Office documents. The *filetype* operator can help you search for these types of files.

More specifically, *filetype* searches for pages that end in a particular file extension. The file extension is the part of the URL following the last period of the filename but before the question mark that begins the parameter list. Since the file extension can indicate what type of program opens a file, the *filetype* operator can be used to search for specific types of files by searching for a specific file extension.

So much has changed in the ten plus years since this process was run for the first edition of this book. Just look at how many more hits Google is reporting! The jump in hits is staggering. If you're unfamiliar with some of these extensions, check out www.filext.com, a great resource for getting detailed information about file extensions, what they are, and what programs they are associated with.

Google converts every document it searches to either HTML or text for online viewing. You can see that Google has searched and converted a file by looking at the results page shown in Figure 2.10.

Notice that the first result lists *[DOC]* before the title of the document and a file format of *MicrosoftWord*. This indicates that Google recognized the file as a Microsoft Word document. In addition, Google has provided a View as HTML link that, when clicked, will display an HTML approximation of the file, as shown in Figure 2.11.

When you click the link for a document that Google has converted, a header is displayed at the top of the page, indicating that you are viewing the HTML version of the page. A link to the original file is also provided. If you think this looks similar to the cached view of a page, you're right. This *is* the cached version of the original page, converted to HTML.

FIGURE 2.10

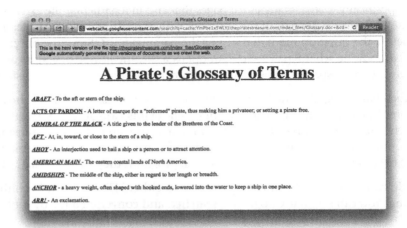

FIGURE 2.11

Although these are great features, Google isn't perfect. Keep these things in mind:

- Google doesn't always provide a link to the converted version of a page.
- Google doesn't always properly recognize the file type of even the most common file formats.
- When Google crawls a page that ends in a particular file extension but that file is blank, Google will sometimes provide a valid file type and a link to the converted page. Even the HTML version of a blank Word document is still, well, blank.

This operator flakes out when ORed. As an example, the query *filetype:doc* returns 39 million results. The query *filetype:pdf* returns 255 million results. The query *(filetype:doc | filetype:pdf)* returns 335 million results, which is pretty close to the two individual search results combined. However, when you start adding to this precocious combination with things like *(filetype:doc | filetpye:pdf) (doc | pdf)*, Google flakes out and returns 441 million results: even more than the original, broader query. I've found that Boolean logic applied to this operator is usually flaky, so beware when you start tinkering.

This operator can be mixed with other operators and search terms.

LINK: SEARCH FOR LINKS TO A PAGE

The *link* operator allows you to search for pages that link to other pages. Instead of providing a search term, the *link* operator requires a URL or server name as an argument. Shown in its most basic form, *link* is used with a server name, as shown in Figure 2.12.

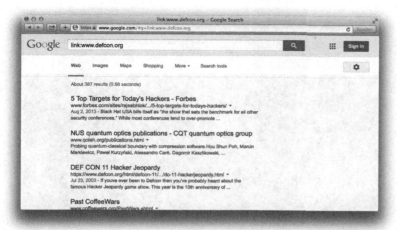

FIGURE 2.12

Each of the search results shown in Figure 2.12 contains HTML links to the http://www.defcon.org Web site. The *link* operator can be extended to include not only basic URLs, but complete URLs that include directory names, file-names, parameters, and the like. Keep in mind that long URLs are much more specific and will return fewer results than their shorter counterparts.

The only place the URL of a link is visible is in the browser's status bar or in the source of the page. For that reason, unlike other cached pages, the cached page for a *link* operator's search result does not highlight the search term, since the search term (the linked Web site) is never really shown in the page. In fact, the cached banner does not make any reference to your search query, as shown in Figure 2.13.

It is a common misconception to think that the *link* operator can actually search for text within a link. The *inanchor* operator performs something similar to this, as we'll see next. To properly use the *link* operator, you must provide a full URL (including protocol, server, directory, and file), a partial URL (in-cluding only the protocol and the host), or simply a server name; otherwise, Google could return unpredictable results. As an example, consider a search for *link:linux*, which returns 151,000 results. This search is not the proper syntax for a link search, since the domain name is invalid. The correct syntax for a search like this might be *link:linux.org* (with 317 results) or *link:linux.org* (with *no* results). These numbers don't seem to make sense, and they certainly don't begin to account for the 151,000 hits on the original query. So what exactly is being returned from Google for a search like *link:linux*? Figure 2.14 shows the answer to this question.

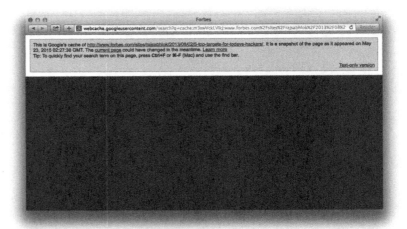

FIGURE 2.13

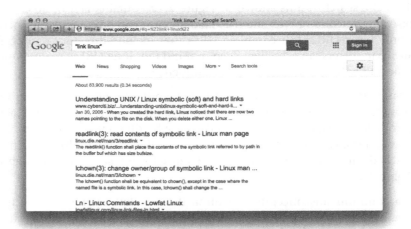

FIGURE 2.14

When an invalid *link:* syntax is provided, Google treats the search as a phrase search. Google offers another clue as to how it handles invalid link searches through the cache page. As shown in Figure 2.15, the cached banner for a site found with a *link:linux* search does not resemble a typical link search cached banner, but rather a standard search cache banner with included highlighted terms.

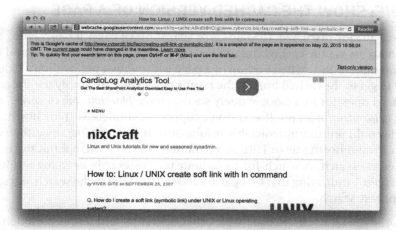

FIGURE 2.15

This is an indication that Google did not perform a link search, but instead treated the search as a phrase, with a colon representing a word break.

The *link* operator cannot be used with other operators or search terms.

INANCHOR: LOCATE TEXT WITHIN LINK TEXT

This operator can be considered a companion to the *link* operator, since they both help search links. The *inanchor* operator, however, searches the text representation of a link, not the actual URL. For example, the Google link to *"current page"* is shown in typical form – as an underlined portion of text. When you click that link, you are taken to the URL http://dmoz.org/Computers/Software/ Operating_Systems/Linux. If you were to look at the actual source of that page, you would see something like this:

<AHREF="http://dmoz.org/Computers/Software/Operating_Systems/Linux/" > current page < /A>

The *inanchor* operator helps search the anchor, or the displayed text on the link, which in this case is the phrase "current page." This is not the same as using *inurl* to find this page with a query like *inurl:Computers inurl:Operating_ Systems*.

Inanchor accepts a word or phrase as an argument, such as *inanchor:click* or *inanchor:James.Foster*. This search will be handy later, especially when we begin to explore ways of searching for relationships between sites. The *inanchor* operator can be used with other operators and search terms.

CACHE: SHOW THE CACHED VERSION OF A PAGE

As we've already discussed, Google keeps snapshots of pages it has crawled that we can access via the cached link on the search results page. If you would like to jump right to the cached version of a page without first performing a Google query to get to the cached link on the results page, you can simply use the *cache* advanced operator in a Google query such as *cache:blackhat.com* or *cache:www. netsec.net/content/index.jsp*. If you don't supply a complete URL or hostname, Google could return unpredictable results. Just as with the *link* operator, passing an invalid hostname or URL as a parameter to *cache* will submit the query as a phrase search. A search for *cache:linux* returns exactly as many results as *"cache linux"*, indicating that Google did indeed treat the cache search as a standard phrase search.

The *cache* operator can be used with other operators and terms, although the results are somewhat unpredictable.

NUMRANGE: SEARCH FOR A NUMBER

The *numrange* operator requires two parameters, a low number and a high number, separated by a dash. This operator is powerful but dangerous when used by malicious Google hackers. As the name suggests, *numrange* can be used to find numbers within a range. For example, to locate the number 12345, a query such as *numrange:12344–12346* will work just fine. When searching for numbers, Google ignores symbols such as currency markers and commas, making it much easier to search for numbers on a page. A shortened version of this operator exists as well. Instead of supplying the *numrange* operator, you can simply provide two numbers in a query, separated by two periods. The shortened version of the query just mentioned would be *12344..12346*. Notice that the *numrange* operator was left out of the query entirely.

This operator can be used with other operators and search terms.

DATERANGE: SEARCH FOR PAGES PUBLISHED WITHIN A CERTAIN DATE RANGE

The *daterange* operator can tend to be a bit clumsy, but it is certainly helpful and worth the effort to understand. You can use this operator to locate pages indexed by Google within a certain date range. Every time Google crawls a page, this date changes. If Google locates some very obscure Web page, it might only crawl it once, never returning to index it again. If you find that your searches are clogged with these types of obscure Web pages, you can remove them from your search (and subsequently get fresher results) through effective use of the *daterange* operator.

The parameters to this operator must always be expressed as a range, two dates separated by a dash. If you only want to locate pages that were indexed on one specific date, you must provide the same date twice, separated by a dash. If this sounds too easy to be true, you're right. It *is* too easy to be true. Both dates passed to this operator must be in the form of two *Julian dates*. The Julian date is the number of days that have passed since January 1, 4713 B.C. For example, the date September 11, 2001, is represented in Julian terms as 2452164. So, to search for pages that were indexed by Google on September 11, 2001, and contained the word *"Osama Bin Laden,"* the query would be *daterange:2452164–2452164 "osama bin laden"*.

Google does not officially support the *daterange* operator, and as such your mileage may vary. Google seems to prefer the date limit used by the advanced search form at www.google.com/advanced_search. As we discussed in the last chapter, this form creates fields in the URL string to perform specific functions. Google designed the *as_qdr* field to help you locate pages that have been *updated* within a certain time frame. For example, to find pages that have been *updated* within the past three months and that contain the word *Google*, use the query *http://www.google.com/search?q=google&as_qdr=m3*. The *info* operator shows the summary information for a site and provides links to other Google searches that might pertain to that site, as shown. The parameter to this operator must be a valid URL or site name. You can achieve this same functionality by supplying a site name or URL as a search query.

This might be a better alternative date restrictor than the clumsy *daterange* operator. Just understand that these are very different functions. *Daterange* is not the advanced-operator equivalent for *as_qdr*, and unfortunately, there is no operator equivalent. If you want to find pages that have been updated within the past year or less, you must either use Google advanced search interface or stick *&as_qdr = 3m* (or equivalent) at the end of your URL.

The *daterange* operator *must* be used with other search terms or advanced operators. It will not return any results when used by itself.

INFO: SHOW GOOGLE'S SUMMARY INFORMATION

The *info* operator shows the summary information for a site and provides links to other Google searches that might pertain to that site, as shown in Figure 2.16. The parameter to this operator must be a valid URL or site name. You can achieve the same functionality by supplying a site name or URL as a search query.

If you don't supply a complete URL or hostname, Google could return unpredictable results. Just as with the *link* and *cache* operators, passing an invalid hostname or URL as a parameter to *info* will submit the query as a phrase

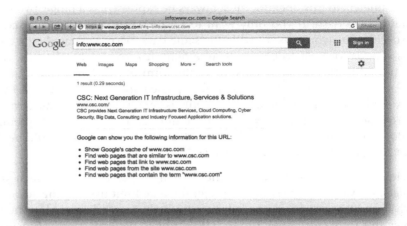

FIGURE 2.16

search. A search for *info:linux* returns exactly as many results as *"info linux,"* indicating that Google did indeed treat the *info* search as a standard phrase search.

The *info* operator cannot be used with other operators or search terms.

RELATED: SHOW RELATED SITES

The *related* operator displays sites that Google has determined are related to a site, as shown in Figure 2.17. The parameter to this operator is a valid site name or URL. You can achieve this same functionality by clicking the "Similar Pages" link from any search results page, or by using the "Find pages similar to the page" portion of the advanced search form.

If you don't supply a complete URL or hostname, Google could return unpredictable results. Passing an invalid hostname or URL as a parameter to *related* will submit the query as a phrase search. A search for *related:linux* returns exactly as many results as *"related linux,"* indicating that Google did indeed treat the cache search as a standard phrase search.

The *related* operator cannot be used with other operators or search terms.

STOCKS: SEARCH FOR STOCK INFORMATION

The *stocks* operator allows you to search for stock market information about a particular company. The parameter to this operator must be a valid stock abbreviation. If you provide a valid stock ticker symbol, you will be taken to a screen that allows further searching for a correct ticker symbol, as shown in Figure 2.18.

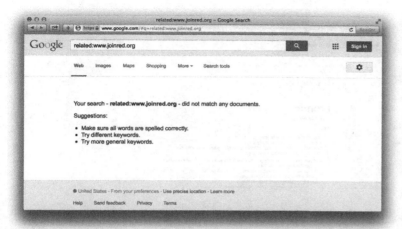

FIGURE 2.17

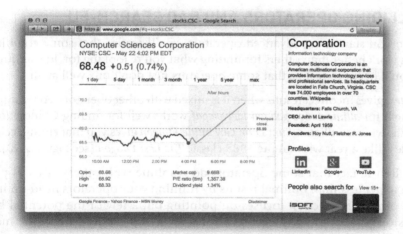

FIGURE 2.18

The *stocks* operator cannot be used with other operators or search terms.

DEFINE: SHOW THE DEFINITION OF A TERM

The *define* operator returns definitions for a search term. Fairly simple, and very straightforward, arguments to this operator may be a word or phrase. Links to the source of the definition are provided, as shown in Figure 2.19.

FIGURE 2.19

COLLIDING OPERATORS AND BAD SEARCH-FU

When you start using advanced operators, you'll realize that some combinations work better than others for finding what you're looking for. Just as quickly, you'll begin to realize that some operators just don't mix well at all.

Allintext gives incorrect results when it is mixed with other operators. For example, a search for *allintext:moo goo gai filetype:pdf* works well for finding Chinese food menus, whereas *allintext:Sum Dum Goy intitle:Dragon* gives you that empty feeling inside – like a year without the 1985 classic *The Last Dragon* (see Figure 2.20).

Despite the fact that some operators do combine with others, it's still possible to get less than optimal results by running your operators head-on into each other. This section focuses on pointing out a few of the potential bad collisions that could give useless results. We'll start with some of the more obvious ones.

First, consider a query like *something – something*. By asking for something and taking away something, we end up with... nothing, and Google tells you as much. This is an obvious example, but consider *intitle:something – intitle:something*. This query, just like the first, returns nothing, since we've negated our first search with a duplicate *NOT* search. Literally, we're saying "find something in the title and hide all the results with something in the title." Both of these examples clearly illustrate the point that you can't query for something and negate that query, because your results will be zero.

It gets bit tricky when the advanced operators start overlapping. Consider *site* and *inurl*. The URL *includes* the name of the site. So, extending the "don't

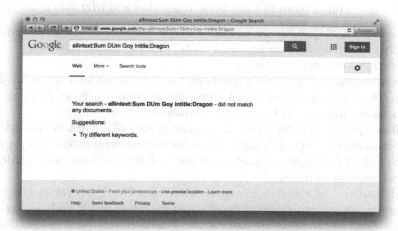

FIGURE 2.20

contradict yourself" rule, don't include a term with *site* and exclude that term with *inurl* and vice versa and expect valid results. A query like *site:microsoft. com -inurl:microsoft.com* doesn't make much sense, and shouldn't work, but as Figure 2.21 shows, it does work.

When you're really trying to home in on a topic, keep the "rules" in mind and you'll accelerate toward your target at a much faster pace. Save the rule breaking for your required Google hacking license test!

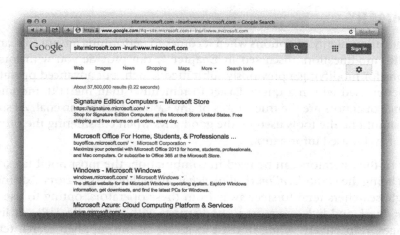

FIGURE 2.21

Here's a quick breakdown of some broken searches and why they're broken:

site:com site:edu – A hit can't be both an *edu* and a *com* at the same time. What you're more likely to search for is *(site:edu | site:com)*, which searches for either domain.

inanchor:click –click – This is contradictory. Remember, unless you use an advanced operator, your search term can appear *anywhere* on the page, including the title, URL, text, and even *anchors*.

allinurl:pdf allintitle:pdf – Operators starting with *all* are notoriously bad at combining. Get out of the habit of combining them before you get *into* the habit of using them! Replace *allinurl* with *inurl*, *allintitle* with *intitle*, and never use *allintext*.

site:*syngress.com allinanchor:syngress publishing* – This query returns zero results, which seems natural considering the last example and the fact that most *all** searches are nasty to use. However, this query suffers from an ordering problem, a fairly common problem that can really throw off some narrow searches. By changing the query to *allinanchor:syngress publishing site:syngress.com*, which moves the *allinanchor* to the beginning of the query, we can get many more results. This does not at all seem natural, since the *allintitle* operator considers all the following terms to be parameters to the operator, but that's just the way it is.

link:www.microsoft.com linux – This is a troublesome search for a beginner because it *appears* to work, finding sites that link to Microsoft and mention the word *linux* on the page. Unfortunately, *link* doesn't mix with other operators, but instead of sending you an error message, Google "fixes" the query for you and provides the exact results as *"link.www. microsoft.com" linux*.

SUMMARY

Google offers plenty of options when it comes to performing advanced searches. URL modification, discussed in Chapter 1, can provide you with lots of options for modifying a previously submitted search, but advanced operators are better used within a query. Easier to remember than the URL modifiers, advance operators are the truest tools of any Google hacker's arsenal. As such, they should be the tools used by the good guys when considering the protection of Web-based information.

Most of the operators can be used in combination, the most notable exceptions being the *allintitle*, *allinurl*, *allinanchor*, and *allintext* operators. Advanced Google searchers tend to steer away from these operators, opting to use the *intitle*, *inurl*, and *link* operators to find strings within the title, URL, or links to pages, respectively. *Allintext*, used to locate all the supplied search terms within the text of a document, is one of the least used and most redundant of the advanced operators. *Filetype* and *site* are very powerful operators that search specific sites or specific file types. The *daterange* operator allows you to search for files that were indexed within a certain time frame, although the URL parameter *as_qdr* seems to be more in vogue. When crawling Web pages, Google generates specific information such as a cached copy of a page, an information snippet about the page, and a list of sites that seem related. This information can be retrieved with the *cache*, *info*, and *related* operators, respectively. The *stocks* operator returns stock information about a specific ticker symbol, whereas the *define* operator returns the definition of a word or simple phrase.

FAST TRACK SOLUTIONS

Intitle
- Finds strings in the title of a page
- Mixes well with other operators
- Best used with Web, Group, Images, and News searches

Allintitle
- Finds all terms in the title of a page
- Does not mix well with other operators or search terms
- Best used with Web, Group, Images, and News searches

Inurl
- Finds strings in the URL of a page
- Mixes well with other operators
- Best used with Web and Image searches

Allinurl
- Finds all terms in the URL of a page
- Does not mix well with other operators or search terms
- Best used with Web, Group, and Image searches

Filetype
- Finds specific types of files based on file extension
- Synonymous with ext
- Requires an additional search term
- Mixes well with other operators
- Best used with Web and Group searches

Allintext
- Finds all provided terms in the text of a page
- Pure evil – don't use it
- Forget you ever heard about *allintext*

Site

- Restricts a search to a particular site or domain
- Mixes well with other operators
- Can be used alone
- Best used with Web, Groups and Image searches

Link

- Searches for links to a site or URL
- Does not mix with other operators or search terms
- Best used with Web searches

Inanchor

- Finds text in the descriptive text of links
- Mixes well with other operators and search terms
- Best used for Web, Image, and News searches

Daterange

- Locates pages indexed within a specific date range
- Requires a search term
- Mixes well with other operators and search terms
- Best used with Web searches
- Might be phased out to make way for *as_qdr*.

Numrange

- Finds a number in a particular range
- Mixes well with other operators and search terms
- Best used with Web searches
- Synonymous with *ext.*

Cache

- Displays Google's cached copy of a page
- Does not mix with other operators or search terms
- Best used with Web searches

Info

- Displays summary information about a page
- Does not mix with other operators or search terms
- Best used with Web searches

Related

- Shows sites that are related to provided site or URL
- Does not mix with other operators or search terms
- Best used with Web searches

Stocks
- Shows the Yahoo Finance stock listing for a ticker symbol
- Does not mix with other operators or search terms
- Best provided as a Web query

Define
- Shows various definitions of a provided word or phrase
- Does not mix with other operators or search terms
- Best provided as a Web query

LINKS TO SITES

- The Google file types FAQ, www.google.com/help/faq_filetypes.html
- The resource for file extension information, www.filext.com. This site can help you figure out what program a particular extension is associated with.
- This article discusses some of the issues associated with Google's date restrict search options. http://searchenginewatch.com/article/2064851/Its-Tough-to-Get-a-Good-Date-with-a-Search-Engine

CHAPTER 3

Google Hacking Basics

INTRODUCTION

A fairly large portion of this book is dedicated to the techniques the "bad guys" will use to locate sensitive information. We present this information to help you become better informed about their motives so that you can protect yourself and perhaps your customers. We've already looked at some of the benign basic searching techniques that are foundational for any Google user who wants to break the barrier of the basics and charge and go to the next level: the ways of the Google hacker. Now we'll start looking at more nefarious uses of Google that hackers are likely to employ.

First, we'll talk about Google's cache. If you haven't already experimented with the cache, you're missing out. I suggest you at least click a few various *cached links* from the Google search results page before reading further. As any decent Google hacker will tell you, there's a certain anonymity that comes with browsing the cached version of a page. That anonymity goes only so far, and there are some limitations to the coverage it provides. Google can, however, very nicely veil your crawling activities to the point that the target Web site might not even get a single packet of data from you as you cruise the Web site. We'll show you how it's done.

Next, we'll talk about directory listings. These "ugly" Web pages are chock full of information, and their mere existence serves as the basis for some of the more advanced attack searches that we'll discuss in later chapters.

To round things out, we'll take a look at a technique that has come to be known as *traversing*: the expansion of a search to try and gather more information. We'll look at directory traversal, number range expansion, and extension trolling, all of which are techniques that should be second nature to any decent hacker – and the good guys that defend against them.

ANONYMITY WITH CACHES

Google's cache feature is truly an amazing thing. The simple fact is that if Google crawls a page or document, you can almost always count on getting a copy of it, even if the original source has since dried up and blown away. Of course the down side of this is that hackers can get a copy of your sensitive data even if you've pulled the plug on that pesky Web server. Another down side of the cache is that the bad guys can crawl your entire Web site (including the areas you "forgot" about) without even sending a single packet to your server. If your Web server doesn't get so much as a packet, it can't write anything to the log files. (You *are* logging your Web connections, aren't you?) If there's nothing in the log files, you might not have any idea that your sensitive data has been carried away. It's sad that we even have to think in these terms, but untold megabytes, gigabytes, and even terabytes of sensitive data leak from Web servers every day. Understanding how hackers can mount an anonymous attack on your sensitive data via Google's cache is of utmost importance.

Google grabs a copy of *most* Web data that it crawls. There are exceptions, and this behavior is preventable, as we'll discuss later, but the vast majority of the data Google crawls is copied and filed away, accessible via the *cached* link on the search page. We need to examine some subtleties to Google's cached document banner. The banner shown in Figure 3.1 was gathered from www. phrack.org.

If you've gotten so familiar with the cache banner that you just blow right past it, slow down a bit and actually read it. The cache banner in Figure 3.2 notes,

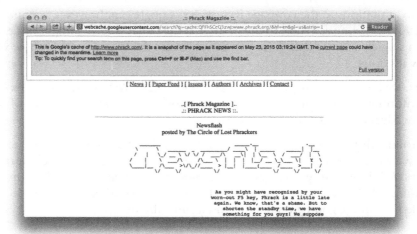

FIGURE 3.1

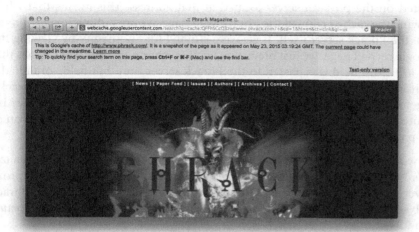

FIGURE 3.2

"This cached page may reference images which are no longer available. "This message is easy to miss, but it provides an important clue about what Google's doing behind the scenes.

To get a better idea of what's happening, let's take a look at a snippet of *tcpdump* output gathered while browsing this cached page. To capture this data, *tcpdump* is simply run as *tcpdump –n*. Your installation or implementation of *tcpdump* might require you to also set a listening interface with the *–i* switch.

Let's take apart this output a bit, starting at the bottom. This is a port 80 (Web) conversation between our browser (10.9.5) and a Google server (66.249.83.83). This is the type of traffic we should expect from any transaction with Google, but the beginning of the capture reveals another port 80 (Web) connection to 200.199.20.162. This is not a Google server, and an *nslookup* of that Internet Protocol (IP) shows that it is the www.phrack.org Web server. The connection to this server can be explained by rerunning *tcpdump* with more options specifically designed to show a few hundred bytes of the data inside the packets as well as the headers, and shift-reloading the cached page. Shift-reloading forces most browsers to contact the Web host again, not relying on any caches the browser might be using.

Lines 0x30 and 0x40 show that we are downloading (via a *GET* request) an image file – specifically, a JPG image from the server. Farther along in the network trace, a *Host* field reveals that we are talking to the www.phrack.org Web server. Because of this *Host* header and the fact that this packet was sent to IP address 200.199.20.162, we can safely assume that the Phrack Web server is virtually hosted on the physical server located at that address. This means that when viewing the cached copy of the Phrack Web page, we are pulling images *directly from* the Phrack server itself. If we were striving for anonymity by viewing the Google cached page, we just blew our cover! Furthermore, line 0x90 shows that the *REFERER* field was passed to the Phrack server, and that field contained a Uniform Resource Locator (URL) reference to Google's cached copy of Phrack's page. This means that not only were we *not* anonymous, but our browser informed the Phrack Web server that we were trying to view a cached version of the page! So much for anonymity.

It's worth noting that most real hackers use proxy servers when browsing a target's Web pages, and even their Google activities are first bounced off a proxy server. If we had used an anonymous proxy server for our testing, the Phrack Web server would have gotten our proxy server's IP address only, not our *actual* IP address.

The cache banner does, however, provide an option to view only the data that Google has captured, without any external references. Despite the fact that we loaded the same page as before, this time we communicated only with a Google server (at 216.239.51.104), not any external servers. If we were to look at the URL generated by clicking the "cached text only" link in the cached page's header, we would discover that Google appended an interesting parameter, *&strip = 1*. This parameter forces a Google *cache* URL to display only cached text, avoiding any external references. This URL parameter only applies to URLs that refer to a Google cached page.

Pulling it all together, we can browse a cached page with a fair amount of anonymity without a proxy server, using a quick cut and paste and a URL modification. As an example, consider query for *site:phrack.org*. Instead of clicking the cached link, we will right-click the cached link and copy the URL to the Clipboard. Browsers handle this action differently, so use whichever technique works for you to capture the URL of this link.

Once the URL is copied to the Clipboard, paste it into the address bar of your browser, and append the *&strip=1* parameter to the end of the URL. The URL should now look something like http://216.239.51.104/search?q=cache:LBQZIrSkMgUJ:www.phrack.org/+site:phrack.org&hl=en&ct=clnk&cd=1&gl=us&client=safari&strip=1. Press **Enter** after modifying the URL to load the page, and you will be taken to the *stripped version* of the cached page, which has a slightly different banner.

Notice that the stripped cache header reads differently than the standard cache header. Instead of the "This cached page may reference images which are no longer available" line, there is a new line that reads, "Click here for the full cached version with images included." This is an indicator that the current cached page has been stripped of external references. Unfortunately, the stripped page does not include graphics, so the page could look quite different from the original, and in some cases a stripped page might not be legible at all. If this is the case, it never hurts to load up a proxy server and hit the page, but real Google hackers "don't need no steenkin' proxy servers!"

DIRECTORY LISTINGS

A *directory listing* is a type of Web page that lists files and directories that exist on a Web server. Designed to be navigated by clicking directory links, directory listings typically have a title that describes the current directory, a list of files and directories that can be clicked, and often a footer that marks the bottom of the directory listing. Each of these elements is shown in the sample directory listing in Figure 3.3.

Much like an FTP server, directory listings offer a no-frills, easy-install solution for granting access to files that can be stored in categorized folders. Unfortunately, directory listings have many faults, specifically:

- They are not secure in and of themselves. They do not prevent users from downloading certain files or accessing certain directories. This task is often left to the protection measures built into the Web server software or third-party scripts, modules, or programs designed specifically for that purpose.
- They can display information that helps an attacker learn specific technical details about the Web server.

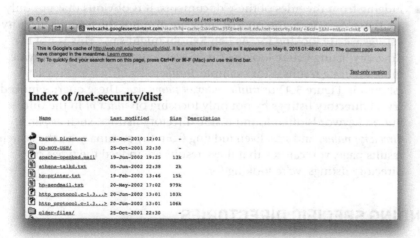

FIGURE 3.3

- They do not discriminate between files that are meant to be public and those that are meant to remain behind the scenes.
- They are often displayed accidentally, since many Web servers display a directory listing if a top-level index file (*index.htm*, *index.html*, *default. asp*, and so on) is missing or invalid.

All this adds up to a deadly combination. In the following section, we'll take a look at some of the ways Google hackers can take advantage of directory listings.

LOCATING DIRECTORY LISTINGS

- The most obvious way an attacker can abuse a directory listing is by simply finding one! Since directory listings offer "parent directory" links and allow browsing through files and folders, even the most basic attacker might soon discover that sensitive data can be found by simply locating the listings and browsing through them.
- Locating directory listings with Google is fairly straightforward. Figure 3.3 shows that most directory listings begin with the phrase "Index of," which also shows in the title. An obvious query to find this type of page might be *intitle:index.of*, which could find pages with the term "index of" in the title of the document. Remember that the period (.) serves as a single-character wildcard in Google. Unfortunately, this query will return a large number of false positives, such as pages with the following titles:
  - Index of Native American Resources on the Internet
  - LibDex – Worldwide index of library catalogues
  - Iowa State Entomology Index of Internet Resources
- Judging from the titles of these documents, it is obvious that not only are these Web pages intentional, they are also not the type of directory listings we are looking for. As Ben Kenobi might say, "This is not the directory listing you're looking for." Several alternate queries provide more accurate results – for example, *intitle:index.of "parent directory"* (shown in Figure 3.4) or *intitle:index.of name size*. These queries indeed reveal directory listings by not only focusing on *index.of* in the title, but on keywords often found inside directory listings, such as *parent directory*, *name*, and *size*. Even judging from the summary on the search results page, you can see that these results are indeed the types of directory listings we're looking for.

FINDING SPECIFIC DIRECTORIES

In some cases, it might be beneficial not only to look for directory listings, but also to look for directory listings that allow access to a specific directory.

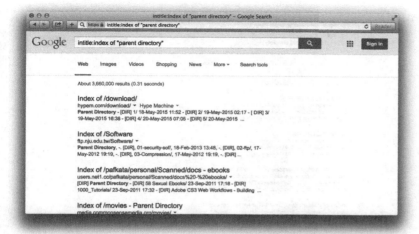

FIGURE 3.4

This is easily accomplished by adding the name of the directory to the search query. To locate "admin" directories that are accessible from directory listings, queries such as *intitle:index.of.admin* or *intitle:index.of inurl:admin* will work well.

FINDING SPECIFIC FILES

Because these types of pages list names of files and directories, it is possible to find very specific files within a directory listing. For example, to find WS_FTP log files, try a search such as *intitle:index.of ws_ftp.log*. This technique can be extended to just about any kind of file by keying in on the *index.of* in the title and the filename in the text of the Web page.

You can also use *filetype* and *inurl* to search for specific files. To search again for *ws_ftp.log* files, try a query like *filetype:log inurl:ws_ftp.log*. This technique will generally find more results than the somewhat restrictive *index.of* search. We'll be working more with specific file searches throughout the book.

SERVER VERSIONING

One piece of information an attacker can use to determine the best method for attacking a Web server is the exact software version. An attacker could retrieve that information by connecting directly to the Web port of that server and issuing a request for the Hypertext Transfer Protocol (HTTP) (Web) headers. It is possible, however, to retrieve similar information from Google without ever

FIGURE 3.5

connecting to the target server. One method involves using the information provided in a directory listing.

Figure 3.5 shows the bottom portion of a typical directory listing. Notice that some directory listings provide the name of the server software as well as the version number. An adept Web administrator could fake these *server tags*, but most often this information is legitimate and exactly the type of information an attacker will use to refine his attack against the server.

The Google query used to locate servers this way is simply an extension of the *intitle:index.of* query. The listing shown was located with a query of *intitle:index. of "server at"*. This query will locate all directory listings on the Web with *index of* in the title and *server at* anywhere in the text of the page. This might not seem like a very specific search, but the results are very clean and do not require further refinement.

To search for a specific server version, the *intitle:index.of* query can be extended even further to something like *intitle:index.of "Apache/1.3.27 Server at"*. This query would find pages like the one listed in Figure 3.5.

In addition to identifying the Web server version, it is also possible to determine the operating system of the server as well as modules and other software that is installed. We'll look at more specific techniques to accomplish this later, but the server versioning technique we've just looked at can be extended by including more details in our query.

One convention used by these sprawling tags is the use of parenthesis to offset the operating system of the server. For example, *Apache/1.3.26 (Unix)* indicates a UNIX-based operating system. Other more specific tags are used as well, some of which are listed below.

- CentOS
- Debian
- Debian GNU/Linux
- Fedora
- FreeBSD
- Linux/SUSE
- Linux/SuSE
- NETWARE
- Red Hat
- Ubuntu
- UNIX
- Win32

An attacker can use the information in these operating system tags in conjunction with the Web server version tag to formulate a specific attack. If this information does not hint at a specific vulnerability, an attacker can still use this information in a data-mining or information-gathering campaign, as we will see in a later chapter.

GOING OUT ON A LIMB: TRAVERSAL TECHNIQUES

The next technique we'll examine is known as *traversal*. Traversal in this context simply means *to travel across*. Attackers use traversal techniques to expand a small "foothold" into a larger compromise.

Directory Traversal

To illustrate how traversal might be helpful, consider a directory listing that was found with *intitle:index.of inurl:"admin"*.

In this example, our query brings us to a relative URL of */admin/php/tour*. If you look closely at the URL, you'll notice an "admin" directory two directory levels above our current location. If we were to click the "parent directory" link, we would be taken up one directory, to the "php" directory. Clicking the "parent directory" link from the "envr" directory would take us to the "admin" directory, a potentially juicy directory. This is very basic directory traversal. We could explore each and every parent directory and each of the subdirectories, looking for juicy stuff. Alternatively, we could use a creative *site* search combined with an *inurl* search to locate a specific file or term inside a specific subdirectory, such as *site:anu.edu inurl:admin ws_ftp.log*, for example. We could also explore this directory structure by modifying the URL in the address bar.

Regardless of how we were to "walk" the directory tree, we would be traversing outside the Google search, wandering around on the target Web server. This is basic traversal, specifically *directory traversal*. Another simple example would be replacing the word *admin* with the word *student* or *public*. Another more serious traversal technique could allow an attacker to take advantage of software flaws to traverse to directories outside the Web server directory tree. For example, if a Web server is installed in the */var/www* directory, and public Web documents are placed in */var/www/htdocs*, by default any user attaching to the Web server's top-level directory is really viewing files located in */var/www/htdocs*. Under normal circumstances, the Web server will not allow Web users to view files above the */var/www/htdocs* directory. Now, let's say a poorly coded third-party software product is installed on the server that accepts directory names as arguments. A normal URL used by this product might be *www.some-sadsite.org/badcode.pl?page=/index.html*. This URL would instruct the *badcode.pl* program to "fetch" the file located at */var/www/htdocs/index.html* and display it to the user, perhaps with a nifty header and footer attached. An attacker might attempt to take advantage of this type of program by sending a URL such as *www.somesad-site.org/badcode.pl?page=../../../etc/passwd*. If the *badcode.pl* program is vulnerable to a directory traversal attack, it would break out of the */var/www/htdocs* directory, crawl up to the *real root* directory of the server, dive down into the */etc* directory, and "fetch" the system password file, displaying it to the user with a nifty header and footer attached!

Automated tools can do a much better job of locating these types of files and vulnerabilities, if you don't mind all the noise they create. If you're a programmer, you will be very interested in the Libwhisker Perl library, written and maintained by Rain Forest Puppy (RFP) and available from www.wiretrip.net/rfp. Security Focus wrote a great article on using Libwhisker. That article is available from www.securityfocus.com/infocus/1798. If you aren't a programmer, RFP's Whisker tool, also available from the Wiretrip site, is excellent, as are other tools based on Libwhisker, such as nikto, written by sullo@cirt.net, which is said to be updated even more than the Whisker program itself. Another tool that performs (amongst other things) file and directory mining is Wikto from SensePost that can be downloaded at www.sensepost.com/research/wikto. The advantage of Wikto is that it does not suffer from false positives on Web sites that responds with friendly 404 messages.

Incremental Substitutions

Another technique similar to traversal is *incremental substitution*. This technique involves replacing numbers in a URL in an attempt to find directories or files that are hidden, or unlinked from other pages. Remember that Google generally only locates files that are linked from other pages, so if it's not linked, Google won't find it. (Okay, there's an exception to every rule. See the FAQ at the end of this chapter.) As a simple example, consider a document called *exhc-1.xls*, found with Google. You could easily modify the URL for that document, changing the 1 to a 2, making the filename *exhc-2.xls*. If the document is found, you have successfully used the incremental substitution technique! In some cases it might be simpler to use a Google query to find other similar files on the site, but remember, not all files on the Web are in Google's databases. Use this technique only when you're sure a simple query modification won't find the files first.

This technique does not apply only to filenames, but just about anything that contains a number in a URL, even parameters to scripts. Using this technique to toy with parameters to scripts is beyond the scope of this book, but if you're interested in trying your hand at some simple file or directory substitutions, look up some test sites with queries such as *filetype:xls inurl:1.xls* or *intitle:index. of inurl:0001* or even an images search for *1.jpg*. Now use substitution to try to modify the numbers in the URL to locate other files or directories that exist on the site. Here are some examples:

- /docs/bulletin/**1.xls** could be modified to /docs/bulletin/**2.xls**
- /DigLib_thumbnail/spmg/hel/**0001**/H/ could be changed to/DigLib_thumbnail/spmg/hel/**0002**/H/
- /gallery/wel008-**1.jpg** could be modified to /gallery/wel008-**2.jpg**

Extension Walking

We've already discussed file extensions and how the *filetype* operator can be used to locate files with specific file extensions. For example, we could easily search for HTM files with a query such as *filetype:HTM1*. Once you've located HTM files, you could apply the substitution technique to find files with the same file name and different extension. For example, if you found */docs/index. htm*, you could modify the URL to */docs/index.asp* to try to locate an *index.asp* file in the *docs* directory. If this seems somewhat pointless, rest assured, this is, in fact, rather pointless. We can, however, make more intelligent substitutions. Consider the directory listing. This listing shows evidence of a very common practice, the creation of backup copies of Web pages.

Backup files can be a very interesting find from a security perspective. In some cases, backup files are older versions of an original file. Backup files on the Web have an interesting side effect: they have a tendency to reveal source code. Source code of a Web page is quite a find for a security practitioner, because it can contain behind-the-scenes information about the author, the code creation and revision process, authentication information, and more.

To see this concept in action, consider the directory listing. Clicking the link for *index.php* will display that page in your browser with all the associated graphics and text, just as the author of the page intended. If this were an HTM or HTML file, viewing the source of the page would be as easy as right-clicking the page and selecting *view source*. PHP files, by contrast, are first *executed* on the server. The results of that executed program are then sent to your browser in the form of HTML code, which your browser then displays. Performing a *view source* on HTML code that was generated from a PHP script *will not* show you the PHP source code, only the HTML. It is not possible to view the actual PHP source code unless something somewhere is misconfigured. An example of such a misconfiguration would be *copying* the PHP code to a filename that ends in something other than PHP, like BAK. Most Web servers do not understand what a BAK file is. Those servers, then, will display a PHP.BAK file as text. When this happens, the actual PHP source code is displayed as text in your browser. PHP source code can be quite revealing, showing things like Structured Query Language (SQL) queries that list information about the structure of the SQL database that is used to store the Web server's data.

The easiest way to determine the names of backup files on a server is to locate a directory listing using *intitle:index.of* or to search for specific files with queries such as *intitle:index.of index.php.bak* or *inurl:index.php.bak*. Directory listings are fairly uncommon, especially among corporate-grade Web servers. However, remember that Google's cache captures a snapshot of a page in time. Just because a Web server isn't hosting a directory listing now, doesn't mean the site never displayed a directory listing. One page was found in Google's cache and was displayed as a directory listing because an *index.php* (or similar file) was missing. In this case, if you were to visit the server on the Web, it would look like a normal page because the index file has since been created. Clicking the cache link, however, shows this directory listing, leaving the list of files on the server exposed. This list of files can be used to intelligently locate files that still most likely exist on the server (via URL modification) without guessing at file extensions.

Directory listings also provide insight into the file extensions that are in use in other places on the site. If a system administrator or Web authoring program creates backup files with a *.BAK* extension in one directory, there's a good chance that BAK files will exist in other directories as well.

SUMMARY

The Google cache is a powerful tool in the hands of the advanced user. It can be used to locate old versions of pages that may expose information that normally would be unavailable to the casual user. The cache can be used to highlight terms in the cached version of a page, even if the terms were not used as part of the query to find that page. The cache can also be used to view a Web page anonymously via the *&strip* = *1* URL parameter, and can be used as a basic transparent proxy server. An advanced Google user will always pay careful attention to the details contained in the cached page's header, since there can be important information about the date the page was crawled, the terms that were found in the search, whether the cached page contains external images, links to the original page, and the text of the URL used to access the cached version of the page. Directory listings provide unique behind-the-scenes views of Web servers, and directory traversal techniques allow an attacker to poke around files that may not be intended for public view.

FAST TRACK SOLUTIONS

Anonymity With Caches

- Clicking the cache link will not only load the page from Google's database, it will also connect to the real server to access graphics and other non-HTML content.
- Adding *&strip = 1* to the end of a cached URL will only show the HTML of a cached page. Accessing a cached page in this way will not connect to the real server on the Web, and could protect your anonymity if you use the cut and paste method shown in this chapter.

Locating Directory Listings

- Directory listings contain a great deal of invaluable information.
- The best way to home in on pages that contain directory listings is with a query such as *intitle:index.of "parent directory"* or *intitle:index.of name size*.

Locating Specific Directories in a Listing

- You can easily locate specific directories in a directory listing by adding a directory name to an *index.of* search. For example, *intitle:index.of inurl:backup* could be used to find directory listings that have the word *backup* in the URL. If the word *backup* is in the URL, there's a good chance it's a directory name.

Locating Specific Files in a Directory Listing

- You can find specific files in a directory listing by simply adding the filename to an *index.of* query, such as *intitle:index.of ws_ftp.log*.

Server Versioning With Directory Listings

- Some servers, specifically Apache and Apache derivatives, add a server tag to the bottom of a directory listing. These server tags can be located by extending an *index.of* search, focusing on the phrase *server at* – for example, *intitle:index.of server.at*.

■ You can find specific versions of a Web server by extending this search with more information from a correctly formatted server tag. For example, the query *intitle:index.of server.at "Apache Tomcat/"* will locate servers running various versions of the Apache Tomcat server.

Directory Traversal

■ Once you have located a specific directory on a target Web server, you can use this technique to locate other directories or subdirectories.

■ An easy way to accomplish this task is via directory listings. Simply click the *parent directory* link, which will take you to the directory above the current directory. If this directory contains another directory listing, you can simply click links from that page to explore other directories. If the parent directory does not display a directory listing, you might have to resort to a more difficult method, guessing directory names and adding them to the end of the parent directory's URL. Alternatively, consider using *site* and *inurl* keywords in a Google search.

Incremental Substitution

■ Incremental substitution is a fancy way of saying "take one number and replace it with the next higher or lower number."

■ This technique can be used to explore a site that uses numbers in directory or filenames. Simply replace the number with the next higher or lower number, taking care to keep the rest of the file or directory name identical (watch those zeroes!). Alternatively, consider using site with either *inurl* or *filetype* keywords in a creative Google search.

Extension Walking

■ This technique can help locate files (for example, backup files) that have the same filename with a different extension.

■ The easiest way to perform extension walking is by replacing one extension with another in a URL – replacing *html* with *bak*, for example.

■ Directory listings, especially cached directory listings, are easy ways to determine whether backup files exist and what kinds of file extensions might be used on the rest of the site.

CHAPTER 4

Document Grinding
and Database Digging

INTRODUCTION

There's no shortage of documents on the Internet. Good guys and bad guys alike can use information found in documents to achieve their distinct purposes. In this chapter we take a look at the ways you can use Google to not only locate these documents but to search within these documents to locate information. There are so many different types of documents and we can't cover them all, but we'll look at the documents in distinct categories based on their function. Specifically, we'll take a look at configuration files, log files, and office documents. Once we've looked at distinct file types, we'll delve into the realm of database digging. We won't examine the details of the Structured Query Language (SQL) or database architecture and interaction; rather, we'll look at the many ways Google hackers can locate and abuse database systems armed with nothing more than a search engine.

One important thing to remember about document digging is that Google will only search the *rendered*, or visible, view of a document. For example, consider a Microsoft Word document. This type of document can contain *metadata*, as shown in Figure 4.1. These fields include such things as the subject, author, manager, company, and much more. Google will not search these fields. If you're interested in getting to the metadata within a file, you'll have to download the actual file and check the metadata yourself.

CONFIGURATION FILES

Configuration files store program settings. An attacker (or security specialist) can use these files to glean insight into the way a program is used and perhaps, by extension, into how the system or network it is operating on is used or configured. As we've seen in previous chapters, even the smallest bit of information can be of interest to a skilled attacker.

61

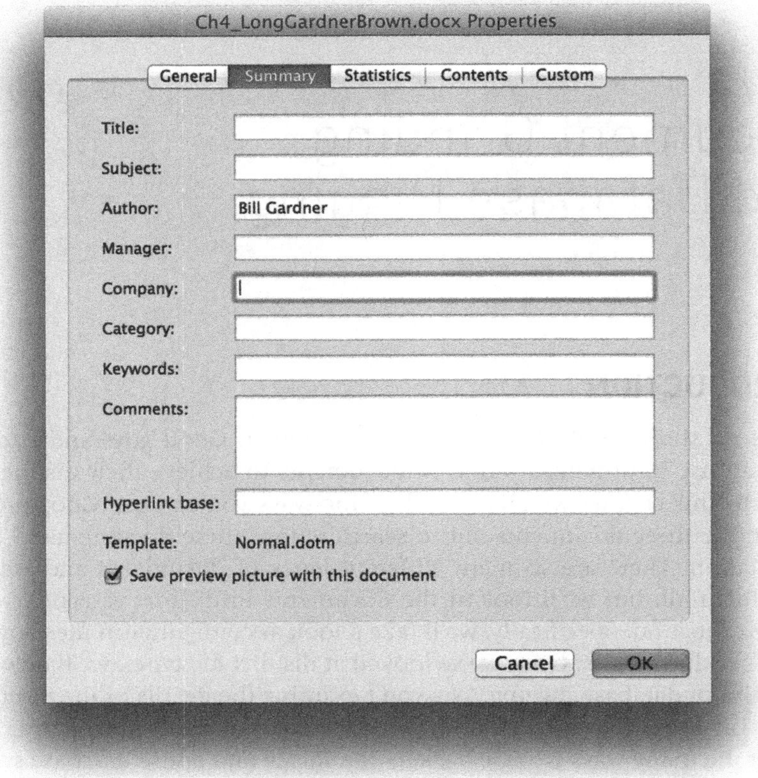

FIGURE 4.1

Consider the file shown in Figure 4.2. This file, found with a query such as *filetype:ini inurl:ws_ftp*, is a configuration file used by the WS_FTP client program. When the WS_FTP program is downloaded and installed, the configuration file contains nothing more than a list of popular, public Internet FTP servers. However, over time, this configuration file can be automatically updated to include the name, directory, username, and password of FTP servers the user connects to. Although the password is encoded when it is stored, some free programs can crack these passwords with relative ease.

Regardless of the type of data in a configuration file, sometimes the mere existence of a configuration file is significant. If a configuration file is located on a server, there's a chance that the accompanying program is installed somewhere on that server or on neighboring machines on the network. Although this might not seem like a big deal in the case of FTP client software, consider a search like *filetype:conf inurl:firewall*, which can locate generic firewall configuration files. This example demonstrates one of the most generic naming

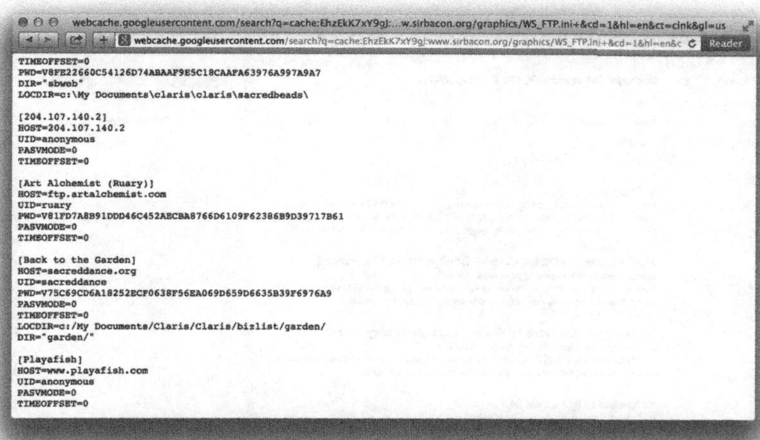
webcache.googleusercontent.com/search?q=cache:EhzEkK7xY9gJ:...w.sirbacon.org/graphics/WS_FTP.ini+&cd=1&hl=en&ct=clnk&gl=us
webcache.googleusercontent.com/search?q=cache:EhzEkK7xY9gJ:www.sirbacon.org/graphics/WS_FTP.ini+&cd=1&hl=en&c
Reader
TIMEOFFSET=0
PWD=V8FE22660C54126D74ABAAF9E5C18CAAFA63976A997A9A7
DIR="sbweb"
LOCDIR=c:\My Documents\claris\claris\sacredbeads\
[204.107.140.2]
HOST=204.107.140.2
UID=anonymous
PASVMODE=0
TIMEOFFSET=0
[Art Alchemist (Ruary)]
HOST=ftp.artalchemist.com
UID=ruary
PWD=V81FD7A8B91DDD46C452AECBA8766D6109F62386B9D39717B61
PASVMODE=0
TIMEOFFSET=0
[Back to the Garden]
HOST=sacreddance.org
UID=sacreddance
PWD=V75C69CD6A18252ECF0638F56EA069D659D6635B39F6976A9
PASVMODE=0
TIMEOFFSET=0
LOCDIR=c:/My Documents/Claris/Claris/bizlist/garden/
DIR="garden/"
[Playafish]
HOST=www.playafish.com
UID=anonymous
PASVMODE=0
TIMEOFFSET=0

FIGURE 4.2

conventions for a configuration file, the use of the *conf* file extension. Other generic naming conventions can be combined to locate other equally common naming conventions. One of the most common base searches for locating configuration files is simply *(inurl:conf OR inurl:config OR inurl:cfg)*, which incorporates the three most common configuration file prefixes. You may also opt to use the *filetype* operator.

If an attacker knows the name of a configuration file as it shipped from the software author or vendor, he can simply create a search targeting that filename using the *filetype* and *inurl* operators. However, most programs allow you to reference a configuration file of any name, making a Google search slightly more difficult. In these cases, it helps to get an idea of the *contents* of the configuration file, which could be used to extract unique strings for use in an effective base search. Sometimes, combining a generic base search with the name (or acronym) of a software product can have satisfactory results, as a search for *(inurl:conf OR inurl:config OR inurl:cfg) MRTG* shows in Figure 4.3.

Although this first search is not far off the mark, it's fairly common for even the best config file search to return page after page of sample or example files, like the sample MRTG configuration file shown in Figure 4.4.

This brings us back, once again, to perhaps the most valuable weapon in a Google hacker's arsenal: effective search reduction. Here's a list of the most common points a Google hacker considers when trolling for configuration files:

- Create a strong base search using unique words or phrases from live files.
- Filter out the words *sample, example, test, how to,* and *tutorial* to narrow the obvious example files.
- Filter out CVS repositories, which often house default config files, with *–cvs*.

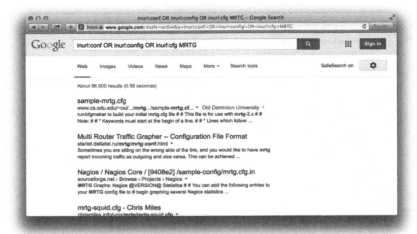

FIGURE 4.3

FIGURE 4.4

- Filter out *manpage* or *Manual* if you're searching for a UNIX program's configuration file.
- Locate the one most commonly changed field in a sample configuration file and perform a negative search on that field, reducing potentially "lame" or sample files.
- To illustrate these points, consider the search *filetype:cfg mrtg "target[*]" -sample -cvs –example*, which locates potentially live MRTG files. As shown in Figure 4.5, this query uses a unique string *"target[*]"* (which is a bit ubiquitous to Google, but still a decent place to start) and removes potential example and CVS files, returning decent results.

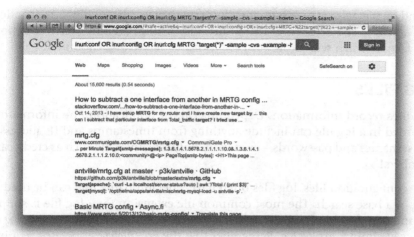

FIGURE 4.5

Some of the results shown in Figure 4.5 might not be real, live MRTG configuration files, but they all have potential, with the exception of the first hit, located in "/Squid-Book."

There's a good chance that this is a sample file, but because of the reduction techniques we've used, the other results are potentially live, production MRTG configuration files.

There is a list of searches that locate various configuration files. These entries were gathered by the many contributors to the GHDB (https://www.exploit-db.com/google-hacking-database/. This list highlights the various methods that can be used to target configuration files. You'll see examples of CVS reduction, sample reduction, unique word and phrase isolation, and more. Most of these queries took imagination on the part of the creator and in many cases took several rounds of reduction by several searchers to get to the query you see here. Learn from these queries, and try them out for yourself. It might be helpful to remove some of the qualifiers, such as *-cvs* or *-sample*, where applicable, to get an idea of what the "messy" version of the search might look like.

LOCATING FILES

To locate files, it's best to try different types of queries. For example, *intitle:index. of ws_ftp.ini* will return results, but so will *filetype:ini inurl:ws_ftp.ini*. The *inurl* search, however, is often the better choice. First, the *filetype* search allows you to browse right to a cached version of the page. Second, the directory listings found by the *index.of* search might allow you to view a list of files but not allow you access to the actual file. Third, directory listings are not overly common. The *filetype* search will locate your file *no matter how* Google found it.

LOG FILES

Log files record information. Depending on the application, the information recorded in a log file can include anything from timestamps and IP addresses to usernames and passwords – even incredibly sensitive data such as credit card numbers!

Like configuration files, log files often have a default name that can be used as part of a base search. The most common file extension for a log file is simply *log*, making the simplest base search for log files simply *filetype:log inurl:log* or the even simpler *ext:log log*. Remember that the *ext (filetype)* operator requires at least one search argument. Log file searches seem to return fewer samples and example files than configuration file searches, but search reduction is still required in some cases. Refer to the rules for configuration file reduction listed previously.

There is also a collection of log file searches collected from the GHDB. These searches show the various techniques that are employed by Google hackers and serve as an excellent learning tool for constructing your own searches during a penetration test.

Log files reveal various types of information, as shown in the search for *filetype:log user- name putty* in Figure 4.6. This log file lists machine names and associated usernames that could be reused in an attack against the machine.

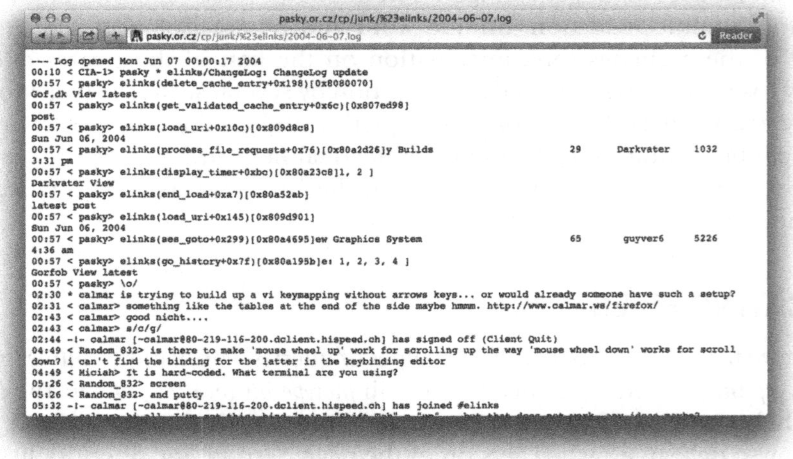

FIGURE 4.6

OFFICE DOCUMENTS

The term *office document* generally refers to documents created by word processing software, spreadsheet software, and lightweight database programs. Common word processing software includes Microsoft Word, Corel WordPerfect, MacWrite, and Adobe Acrobat. Common spreadsheet programs include Microsoft Excel, Lotus 1-2-3, and Linux's Gnumeric. Other documents that are generally lumped together under the office document category include Microsoft PowerPoint, Microsoft Works, and Microsoft Access documents.

In many cases, simply searching for these files with *filetype* is pointless without an additional specific search. Google hackers have successfully uncovered all sorts of interesting files by simply throwing search terms such as *private* or *password* or *admin* onto the tail end of a *filetype* search. However, simple base searches such as *(inurl:xls OR inurl:doc OR inurl:mdb)* can be used as a broad search across many file types.

Some searches, such as *filetype:xls inurl:password.xls*, focus on a file with a specific name. The *password.xls* file does not necessarily belong to any specific software package, but it sounds interesting simply because of the name. Other searches, such as *filetype:xls username password email*, shift the focus from the file's name to its contents. The reasoning here is that if an Excel spreadsheet contains the words *username password* and *email*, there's a good chance the spreadsheet contains sensitive data such as passwords. The heart and soul of a good Google search involves refining a generic search to uncover something extremely relevant. Google's ability to search inside different types of documents is an extremely powerful tool in the hands of an advanced Google user.

DATABASE DIGGING

There has been intense focus recently on the security of Web-based database applications, specifically the front–end software that interfaces with a database. Within the security community, talk of SQL injection has all but replaced talk of the once-common CGI vulnerability, indicating that databases have arguably become a greater target than the underlying operating system or Web server software.

An attacker will not generally use Google to *break into* a database or muck with a database front–end application; rather, Google hackers troll the Internet looking for bits and pieces of database information leaked from potentially vulnerable servers. These bits and pieces of information can be used to first select a target and then to mount a more educated attack (as opposed to a ground-zero blind attack) against the target. Bearing this in mind, understand that here we do not discuss the actual mechanics of the attack itself, but rather the surprisingly invasive information-gathering phase an accomplished Google hacker will employ prior to attacking a target.

LOGIN PORTALS

A login portal is the "front door" of a Web-based application. Proudly displaying a username and password dialog, login portals generally bear the scrutiny of most Web attackers simply because they are the one part of an application that is most carefully secured. There are obvious exceptions to this rule, but as an analogy, if you're going to secure your home, aren't you going to first make sure your front door is secure?

A typical database login portal is shown in Figure 4.7. This login page announces not only the existence of an SQL server but also the Microsoft Web Data Administrator software package.

Regardless of its relative strength, the mere existence of a login portal provides a glimpse into the type of software and hardware that might be employed at a target. Put simply, a login portal is terrific for footprinting. In extreme cases, an unsecured login portal serves as a welcome mat for an attacker. To this end, let's look at some queries that an attacker might use to locate database front ends on the Internet.

One way to locate login portals is to focus on the word *login*. Another way is to focus on the copyright at the bottom of a page. Most big-name portals put a copyright notice at the bottom of the page. Combine this with the product name, and a *welcome* or two, and you're off to a good start.

SUPPORT FILES

Another way an attacker can locate or gather information about a database is by querying for support files that are installed with, accompany, or are created by the database software. These can include configuration files, debugging

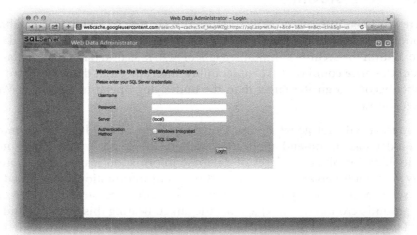

FIGURE 4.7

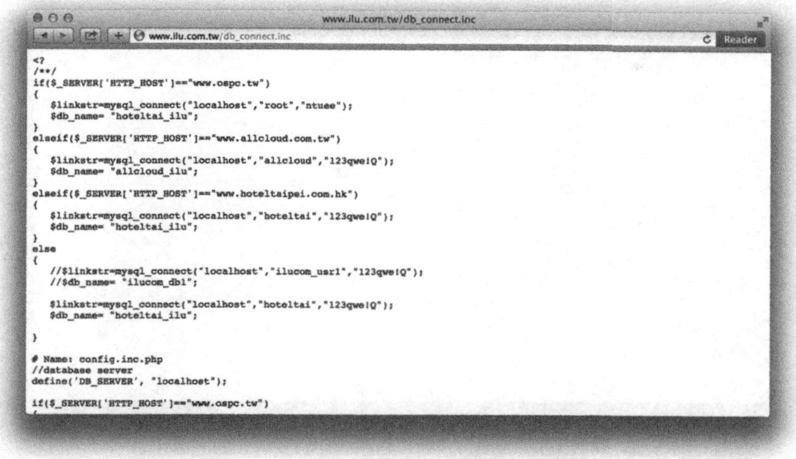

FIGURE 4.8

scripts, and even sample database files. Some searches locate specific support files that are included with or are created by popular database clients and servers. As an example of a support file, PHP scripts using the *mysql_connect* function reveal machine names, usernames, and cleartext passwords, as shown in Figure 4.8. Strictly speaking, this file contains PHP code, but the INC extension makes it an *include file*. It's the content of this file that is of interest to a Google hacker.

ERROR MESSAGES

As we've discussed throughout this book, error messages can be used for all sorts of profiling and information-gathering purposes. Error messages also play a key role in the detection and profiling of database systems. As is the case with most error messages, database error messages can also be used to profile the operating system and Web server version. Conversely, operating system and Web server error messages can be used to profile and detect database servers.

In addition to revealing information about the database server, error messages can also reveal much more dangerous information about potential vulnerabilities that exist in the server. For example, consider an error such as *"SQL command not properly ended"*, displayed in Figure 4.9. This error message indicates that a terminating character was not found at the end of an SQL statement. If a command accepts user input, an attacker could leverage the information in this error message to execute an SQL injection attack.

FIGURE 4.9

DATABASE DUMPS

The output of a database into any format can be constituted as a database dump. For the purposes of Google hacking, however, we'll use the term *database dump* to describe the text-based conversion of a database. As we'll see next in this chapter, it's entirely possible for an attacker to locate just about any type of binary database file, but standardized formats (such as the text-based SQL dump shown in Figure 4.10) are very commonplace on the Internet.

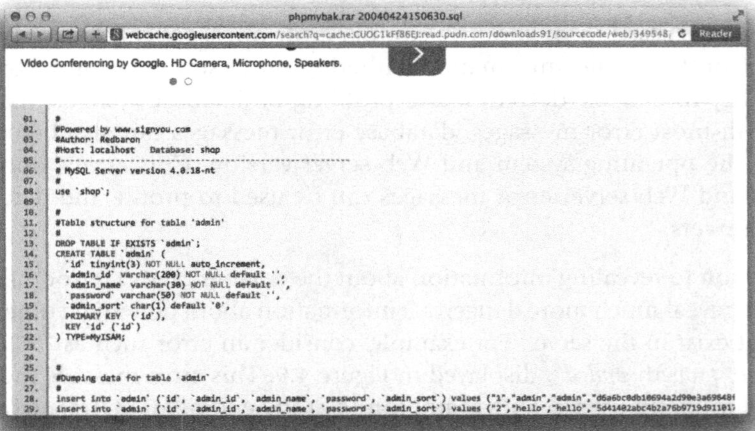

FIGURE 4.10

Using a full database dump, a database administrator can completely rebuild a database. This means that a full dump details not only the structure of the database's tables but also every record in each and every table. Depending on the sensitivity of the data contained in the database, a database dump can be very revealing and obviously makes a terrific tool for an attacker. There are several ways an attacker can locate database dumps. One of the most obvious ways is by focusing on the headers of the dump, resulting in a query such as *"#Dumping data for table"*, as shown in Figure 4.10. This technique can be expanded to work on just about any type of database dump headers by simply focusing on headers that exist in every dump and that are unique phrases that are unlikely to produce false positives.

Specifying additional specific interesting words or phrases such as *username*, *password*, or *user* can help narrow this search. For example, if the word *password* exists in a database dump, there's a good chance that a password of some sort is listed inside the database dump. With proper use of the *OR* symbol (|), an attacker can craft an extremely effective search, such as *"# Dumping data for table"* *(user | username | pass | password)*. In addition, an attacker could focus on file extensions that some tools add to the end of a database dump by querying for *filetype:sql sql* and further narrowing to specific words, phrases, or sites. The SQL file extension is also used as a generic description of batched SQL commands.

ACTUAL DATABASE FILES

Another way an attacker can locate databases is by searching directly for the database itself. This technique does not apply to all database systems, only those systems in which the database is represented by a file with a specific name or extension. Be advised that Google will most likely not understand how to process or translate these files, and the summary (or snippet) on the search result page will be blank and Google will list the file as an "unknown type," as shown in Figure 4.11.

If Google does not understand the format of a binary file, as with many of those located with the *filetype* operator, you will be unable to search for strings *within* that file. This considerably limits the options for effective searching, forcing you to rely on *inurl* or *site* operators instead.

AUTOMATED GRINDING

Searching for files is fairly straightforward – especially if you know the type of file you're looking for. We've already seen how easy it is to locate files that contain sensitive data, but in some cases it might be necessary to search files offline. For example, assume that we want to troll for yahoo.com email addresses. A query such as *"@yahoo.com"* *email* is not at all effective as a Web search, and even as a Group search it is problematic, as shown in Figure 4.12.

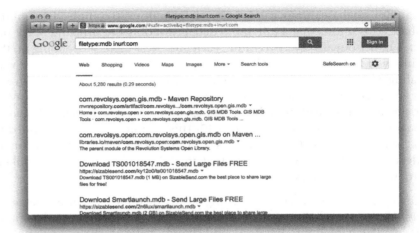

FIGURE 4.11

This search located one email address, *jg65_83@yahoo.com*, but also keyed on *store.yahoo.com*, which is not a valid email address. In cases like this, the best option for locating specific strings lies in the use of *regular expressions*. This involves downloading the documents you want to search (which you most likely found with a Google search) and parsing those files for the information you're looking for. You could opt to automate the process of downloading these files, as we'll show in Chapter 12, but once you have downloaded the files, you'll

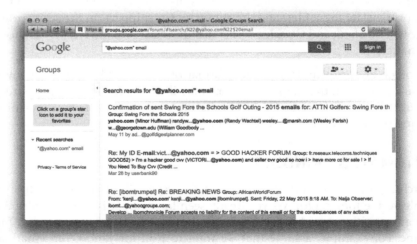

FIGURE 4.12

need an easy way to search the files for interesting information. Consider the following Perl script:

```perl
#!/usr/bin/perl
#
# Usage: ./ssearch.pl FILE_TO_SEARCH WORDLIST
#
# Locate words in a file, coded by James Foster
#
use strict;

open(SEARCHFILE,$ARGV[0]) || die("Can not open searchfile because $!");

open(WORDFILE,$ARGV[1]) || die("Can not open wordfile because $!");

my @WORDS=<WORDFILE>;

close(WORDFILE);

my $LineCount = 0;

while(<SEARCHFILE>) {

  foreach my $word (@WORDS) {

close(SEARCHFILE);
```

This script accepts two arguments: a file to search and a list of words to search for. As it stands, this program is rather simplistic, acting as nothing more than a glorified *grep* script. However, the script becomes much more powerful when instead of words, the word list contains regular expressions. For example, consider the following regular expression, written by Don Ranta:

```
[a-zA-Z0-9._-]+@(([a-zA-Z0-9_-]{2,99}\.)+[a-zA-Z]{2,4})|((25[0-5]|2[0-
4]\d|1\d\d|[1-9]\d|[1-9])\.(25[0-5]|2[0-4]\d|1\d\d|[1-9]\d|[1-9])\.(25[0-5]|2[0-
4]\d|1\d\d|[1-9]\d|[1-9])\.(25[0-5]|2[0-4]\d|1\d\d|[1-9]\d|[1-9])))
```

Unless you're somewhat skilled with regular expressions, this might look like a bunch of garbage text. This regular expression is very powerful, however, and will locate various forms of email address.

Let's take a look at this regular expression in action. For this example, we'll save the results of a Google Groups search for *"@yahoo.com" email* to a file called results.html, and we'll enter the preceding regular expression all on one line of a file called wordfile.txt. We can also grab the search results from the command line with a program like Lynx, a common text-based Web browser. Other programs could be used instead of Lynx – Curl, Netcat, Telnet, or even "save as" from a standard Web browser. Remember that Google's terms of service frown on any form of automation. In essence, Google prefers that you simply execute your search from the browser, saving the results manually. However, as we've discussed previously, if you honor the *spirit* of the terms of service, taking care not to abuse Google's free search service with excessive automation, the folks at Google will most likely not turn their wrath upon you. Regardless, most people will ultimately decide for themselves how strictly to follow the terms of service.

Back to our Google search. Notice that the URL indicates we're grabbing the first hundred results, as demonstrated by the use of the *num = 100* parameter. This will potentially locate more email addresses. Once the results are saved to the *results.html* file, we'll run our ssearch.pl script against the results.html file, searching for the email expression we've placed in the wordfile.txt file. To help narrow our results, we'll pipe that output into *"grep yahoo | head –15 | sort –u"* to return utmost 15 unique addresses that contain the word *yahoo*. The final (obfuscated) results are shown in Figure 4.13.

As you can see, this combination of commands works fairly well at unearthing email addresses. If you're familiar with UNIX commands, you might

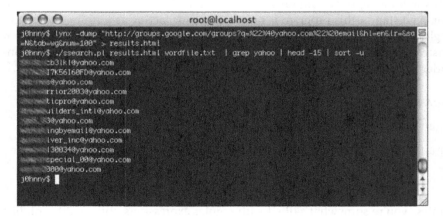

FIGURE 4.13

have already noticed that there is little need for *two* separate commands. This entire process could have been easily combined into one command by modifying the Perl script to read standard input and piping the output from the Lynx command directly into the ssearch.pl script, effectively by-passing the results.html file. Presenting the commands this way, however, opens the door for *irresponsible* automation techniques, which isn't overtly encouraged.

Other regular expressions can come in handy as well. This expression, also by Don Ranta, locates URLs:

[a-zA-Z]{3,4}[sS]?://((([\w\d\-]+\.)+[a-zA-Z]{2,4})|((25[0-5]|2[0-4]\d|1\d\d|[1-

9]\d|[1-9])\.(25[0-5]|2[0-4]\d|1\d\d|[1-9]\d|[1-9])\.(25[0-5]|2[0-4]\d|1\d\d|[1-

9]\d|[1-9])\.(25[0-5]|2[0-4]\d|1\d\d|[1-9]\d|[1-9])))((\?|/)[\w/=+#_~&:;%\-

\?\.]*)*

This expression, which will locate URLs and parameters, including addresses that consist of either IP addresses or domain names, is great at processing a Google results page, returning all the links on the page. This doesn't work as well as the API-based methods, but it is simpler to use than the API method. This expression locates IP addresses:

(25[0-5]|2[0-4]\d|1\d\d|[1-9]\d|[1-9])\.(25[0-5]|2[0-4]\d|1\d\d|[1-9]\d|[1-

9])\.(25[0-5]|2[0-4]\d|1\d\d|[1-9]\d|[1-9])\.(25[0-5]|2[0-4]\d|1\d\d|[1-9]\d|[1-9])

We can use an expression like this to help map a target network. These techniques could be used to parse not only HTML pages but also practically any type of document. However, keep in mind that many files are binary, meaning that they should be converted into text before they're searched. The UNIX *strings* command (usually implemented with *strings −8* for this purpose) works very well for this task, but don't forget that Google has the built-in capability to translate many different types of documents for you. If you're searching for visible text, you should opt to use Google's translation, but if you're searching for nonprinted text such as metadata, you'll need to first download the original file and search it offline. Regardless of how you implement these techniques, it should be clear to you by now that Google can be used as an extremely powerful information-gathering tool when it's combined with even a little automation.

SUMMARY

The subject of document grinding is topic worthy of an entire book. In a single chapter, we can only hope to skim the surface of this topic. An attacker (black or white hat) who is skilled in the art of document grinding can glean loads of information about a target. In this chapter we've discussed the value of configuration files, log files, and office documents, but obviously there are many other types of documents we could focus on as well. The key to document grinding is first discovering the types of documents that exist on a target and then, depending on the number of results, to narrow the search to the more interesting or relevant documents. Depending on the target, the line of business they're in, the document type, and many other factors, various keywords can be mixed with *filetype* searches to locate key documents.

Database hacking is also a topic for an entire book. However, there is obvious benefit to the information Google can provide prior to a full-blown database audit. Login portals, support files, and database dumps can provide various information that can be recycled into an audit. Of all the information that can be found from these sources, perhaps the most telling (and devastating) is source code. Lines of source code provide insight into the way a database is structured and can reveal flaws that might otherwise go unnoticed from an external assessment. In most cases, though, a thorough code review is required to determine application flaws. Error messages can also reveal a great deal of information to an attacker.

Automated grinding allows you to search many documents programmatically for bits of important information. When it's combined with Google's excellent document location features, you've got a very powerful information-gathering weapon at your disposal.

FAST TRACK SOLUTIONS

Configuration Files
- Configuration files can reveal sensitive information to an attacker.
- Although the naming varies, configuration files can often be found with file extensions like INI, CONF, CONFIG, or CFG.

Log Files
- Log files can also reveal sensitive information that is often more current than the information found in configuration files.
- Naming convention varies, but log files can often be found with file extensions like LOG.

Office Documents

- In many cases, office documents are intended for public release. Documents that are inadvertently posted to public areas can contain sensitive information.
- Common office file extensions include PDF, DOC, TXT, or XLS.
- Document content varies, but strings like private, password, backup, or admin can indicate a sensitive document.

Database Digging

- Login portals, especially default portals supplied by the software vendor, are easily searched for and act as magnets for attackers seeking specific versions or types of software. The words *login, welcome,* and *copyright statements* are excellent ways of locating login portals.
- Support files exist for both server and client software. These files can reveal information about the configuration or usage of an application.
- Error messages have varied content that can be used to profile a target.
- Database dumps are arguably the most revealing of all database finds because they include full or partial contents of a database. These dumps can be located by searching for strings in the headers, like *"# Dumping data for table".*

Links to Sites

- **www.filext.com** – A great resource for getting information about file extensions.
- **www.exploit-db.com/google-dorks/** – The home of the Google Hacking Database, where you can find more searches like those listed in this chapter.

Frequently Asked Questions

The following frequently asked questions, answered by the authors of this book, are designed to both measure your understanding of the concepts presented in this chapter and to assist you with real-life implementation of these concepts.

Q: What can I do to help prevent this form of information leakage?

A: To fix this problem on a site you are responsible for, first review all documents available from a Google search. Ensure that the returned documents are, in fact, supposed to be in the public view. Although you might opt to scan your site for database information leaks with an automated tool the best way to prevent this is at the source. Your database remote administration tools should be locked down from outside users, default login portals should be reviewed for safety and checked to ensure that software versioning information has been removed, and support files should be removed from your public servers. Error messages should be tailored to ensure that excessive information is not revealed, and a full application review should be performed on all applications in use. In addition, it doesn't hurt to configure your Web server to only allow certain file types to be downloaded. It's much easier to list the file types you will allow than to list the file types you *don't* allow.

Q: I'm concerned about excessive metadata in office documents. Can I do anything to clean up my documents?

A: Microsoft provides a Web page dedicated to the topic: http://support.microsoft.com/default.aspx?scid{kb;EN-US;Q223396. In addition, several utilities are available to automate the cleaning process.

Q: Many types of software rely on *include files* to pull in external content. As I understand it, include files, like the INC files discussed in this chapter, are a problem because they often reveal sensitive information meant for programs, not Web visitors. Is there any way to resolve the dangers of include files?

A: Include files are in fact a problem because of their file extensions. If an extension such as .INC is used, most Web servers will display them as text, revealing sensitive data. Consider blocking .INC files (or whatever extension you use for includes) from being downloaded. This server modification will keep the file from presenting in a browser but will still allow back-end processes to access the data within the file.

Q: Our software uses .INC files to store database connection settings. Is there another way?

A: Rename the extension to .PHP so that the contents are not displayed.

Q: How can I avoid our application database from being downloaded by a Google hacker?

A: Read the documentation. Some badly written software has hardcoded paths but most allow you to place the file outside the Web server's *docroot*.

CHAPTER 5

Google's Part in an Information Collection Framework

INTRODUCTION

There are various reasons for hacking. When most of us hear hacker we think about computer and network security, but lawyers, salesmen, and policemen are also hackers at heart. It's really a state of mind and a way of thinking rather than a physical attribute. Why do people hack? There are a couple of motivators, but one specific reason is to be able to know things that the ordinary man on the street doesn't. From this many of the other motivators stem out. Knowledge is power – there's a rush to seeing what others are doing without them knowing it. Understanding that the thirst for knowledge is central to hacking, consider Google, a massively distributed supercomputer, with access to all known information and with a deceivingly simple user interface, just waiting to answer any query within seconds. It is almost as if Google was made for hackers.

The first and second editions of this book brought to light many techniques that a hacker (or penetration tester) might use to obtain information that would help him or her in conventional security assessments (e.g., finding networks, domains, email addresses, and so on). During such a conventional security test (or pen test) the aim is almost always to breach security measures and get access to information that is restricted. However, this information can be reached simply by assembling related pieces of information together to form a bigger picture. This, of course, is not true for all information. The chances that I will find your super secret double encrypted document on Google is extremely slim, but you can bet that the way to get to it will eventually involve a lot of information gathering from public sources like Google.

If you are reading this book you are probably already interested in information mining, getting the most from search engines by using them in interesting ways. In this chapter I hope to show interesting and clever ways to do just that.

THE PRINCIPLES OF AUTOMATING SEARCHES

Computers help automate tedious tasks. Clever automation can accomplish what a thousand disparate people working simultaneously cannot. But it's impossible to automate something that cannot be done manually. If you want to write a program to perform something, you need to have done the entire process by hand, and have that process work every time. It makes little sense to automate a flawed process. Once the manual process is ironed out, an algorithm is used to translate that process into a computer program.

Let's look at an example. A user is interested in finding out which Web sites contain the email address *andrew@syngress.com*. As a start, the user opens Google and types the email address in the input box. The results are shown in Figure 5.1.

The user sees that there are three different sites with that email address listed: *g.bookpool.com*, *www.networksecurityarchive.org*, and *book.google.com*. In the back of his or her mind is the feeling that these are not the only sites where the email address appears, and remembers that he or she has seen places where email addresses are listed as *andrew at syngress dot com*. When the user puts this search into Google, he or she gets different results, as shown in Figure 5.2.

Clearly the lack of quotes around the query gave incorrect results. The user adds the quotes and gets the results shown in Figure 5.3.

By formulating the query differently, the user now has a new result: *taosecurity. blogspot.com*. The manipulation of the search query worked, and the user has found another site reference.

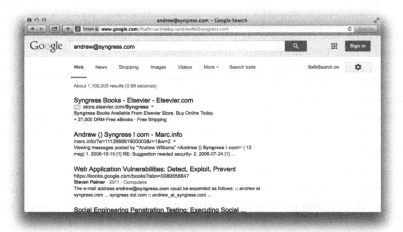

FIGURE 5.1

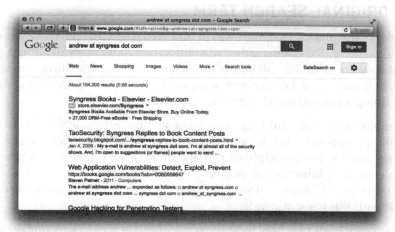

FIGURE 5.2

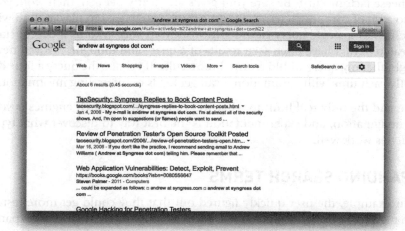

FIGURE 5.3

If we break this process down into logical parts, we see that there are actually many different steps that were followed. Almost all searches follow these steps:

- Define an original search term
- Expand the search term
- Get data from the data source
- Parse the data
- Postprocess the data into information.

Let's look at these in more detail.

THE ORIGINAL SEARCH TERM

The goal of the previous example was to find Web pages that reference a specific email address. This seems rather straightforward, but clearly defining a goal is probably the most difficult part of any search. Brilliant searching won't help attain an unclear goal. When automating a search, the same principles apply as when doing a manual search: garbage in, garbage out.

Computers are bad at "thinking" and good at "number crunching." Don't try to make a computer think for you, because you will be bitterly disappointed with the results. The principle of garbage in, garbage out simply states that if you enter bad information into a computer from the start, you will only get garbage (or bad information) out. Inexperienced search engine users often wrestle with this basic principle.

In some cases, goals may need to be broken down. This is especially true of broad goals, like trying to find email addresses of people that work in cheese factories in the Netherlands. In this case, at least one subgoal exists – you'll need to define the cheese factories first. Be sure your goals are clearly defined, then work your way to a set of core search terms. In some cases, you'll need to play around with the results of a single query in order to work your way towards a decent starting search term. I have often seen results of a query and thought, "Wow, I never thought that my query would return these results. If I shape the query a little differently each time with automation, I can get loads of interesting information."

In the end the only real limit to what you can get from search engines is your own imagination, and experimentation is the best way to discover what types of queries work well.

EXPANDING SEARCH TERMS

In our example, the user quickly figured out that they could get more results by changing the original query into a set of slightly different queries. Expanding search terms is fairly natural for humans, and the real power of search automation lies in thinking about that human process and translating it into some form of algorithm. By programmatically changing the standard form of a search into many different searches, we save ourselves from manual repetition, and more importantly, from having to remember all of the expansion tricks. Let's take a look at a few of these expansion techniques.

Email Addresses

Many sites try obscure email addresses in order to fool data-mining programs. This is done for a good reason: the majority of the data-mining programs troll sites to collect email addresses for spammers. If you want a sure fire way to receive a lot of spam, post to a mailing list that does not obscure your email address. While it's a good thing that sites automatically obscure the email address, it also makes our lives as Web searchers difficult. Luckily, there are ways to beat this; however, these techniques are also not unknown to spammers.

When searching for an email address we can use the following expansions. The email address *andrew@syngress.com* could be expanded as follows:

- *andrew at syngress.com*
- *andrew at syngress dot com*
- *andrew@syngress dot com*
- *andrew_at_syngress.com*
- *andrew_at_syngress dot com*
- *andrew_at_syngress_dot_com*
- *andrew@syngress.remove.com*
- *andrew@_removethis_syngress.com*

Note that the "@" sign can be written in many forms (e.g., – (at), _at_ or -at-). The same goes for the dot ("."). You can also see that many people add "remove" or "removethis" in an email address. At the end it becomes an 80/20 thing – you will find 80% of addresses when implementing the top 20% of these expansions.

At this stage you might feel that you'll never find every instance of the address (and you may be right). But there is a tiny light at the end of the tunnel. Google ignores certain characters in a search. A search for *andrew@syngress.com* and *"andrew syngress com"* returns the same results. The @ sign and the dot are simply ignored. So when expanding search terms, don't include both, because you are simply wasting a search.

Verifying an Email Address

Here's a quick hack to verify if an email address exists. While this might not work on all mail servers, it works on the majority of them – including Gmail. Have a look:

- Step 1. Find the mail server: $ host -t mx gmail.com
    - gmail.com mail is handled by 5 gmail-smtp-in.l.google.com.
    - gmail.com mail is handled by 10 alt1.gmail-smtp-in.l.google.com.
    - gmail.com mail is handled by 10 alt2.gmail-smtp-in.l.google.com.
    - gmail.com mail is handled by 50 gsmtp163.google.com.
    - gmail.com mail is handled by 50 gsmtp183.google.com.
- Step 2. Pick one and Telnet to port 25 $ telnet gmail-smtp-in.l.google.com 25
    - Trying 64.233.183.27
    - Connected to gmail-smtp-in.l.google.com.
    - Escape character is "^]".
    - 220 mx.google.com ESMTP d26si15626330nfh

- Step 3. Mimic the Simple Mail Transfer Protocol (SMTP): HELO test
  - 250 mx.google.com at your service
  - MAIL FROM: <test@test.com>
  - 250 2.1.0 OK
- Step 4a. Positive test – RCPT TO: <roelof.temmingh@gmail.com>
  - 250 2.1.5 OK
- Step 4b. Negative test – RCPT TO: <kosie.kramer@gmail.com>
  - 550 5.1.1 No such user d26si15626330nfh
- Step 5. Say goodbye: quit
  - 221 2.0.0 mx.google.com closing connection d26si15626330nfh

By inspecting the responses from the mail server we have now verified that *roelof.temmingh@gmail.com* exists, while *kosie.kramer@gmail.com* does not. In the same way, we can verify the existence of other email addresses.

On Windows platforms you will need to use the *nslookup* command to find the email servers for a domain. You can do this as follows: *nslookup -qtype=mx gmail.com*

Telephone Numbers

While email addresses have a set format, telephone numbers are a different kettle of fish. It appears that there is no standard way of writing down a phone number. Let's assume you have a number that is in South Africa and the number itself is 012 555 1234. The number can appear on the Internet in many different forms:

- 012 555 1234 (local)
- 012 5551234 (local)
- 012555124 (local)
- +27 12 555 1234 (with the country code)
- +27 12 5551234 (with the country code)
- +27 (0)12 555 1234 (with the country code)
- 0027 (0)12 555 1234 (with the country code)

One way of catching all of the results would be to look for the most significant part of the number, "555 1234" and "5551234." However, this has a drawback as you might find that the same number exists in a totally different country, giving you a false positive.

An interesting way to look for results that contain telephone numbers within a certain range is by using Google's *numrange* operator. A shortcut for this is to specify the start number, then ".." followed by the end number. Let's see how this works in real life. Imagine I want to see what results I can find on the area code +1 252 793. You can use the *numrange* operator to specify the query as shown in Figure 5.4.

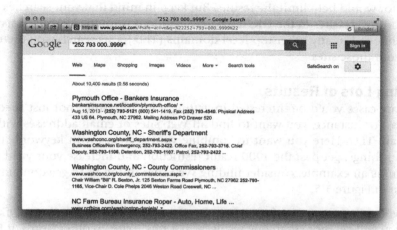

FIGURE 5.4

We can clearly see that the results all contain numbers located in the specified range in North Carolina. We will see how this ability to restrict results to a certain area is very useful later in this chapter.

People

One of the best ways to find information about someone is to Google them. If you haven't Googled for yourself, you are the odd one out. There are many ways to search for a person and most of them are straightforward. If you don't get results straight away don't worry, there are numerous options. Assuming you are looking for Andrew Williams you might search for:

- "Andrew Williams"
- "Williams Andrew"
- "A Williams"
- "Andrew W"
- Andrew Williams
- Williams Andrew

Note that the last two searches do not have quotes around them. This is to find phrases like "Andrew is part of the Williams family".

With a name like Andrew Williams you can be sure to get a lot of false positives as there are probably many people named Andrew Williams on the Internet. As such, you need to add as many additional search terms to your search as possible. For example, you may try something like *"Andrew Williams" Syngress publishing security*. Another tip to reduce false positives is to restrict the site to a particular country. If Andrew stayed in England, adding the *site:uk* operator would help limit the results. But keep in mind that your searches are then limited to sites in the UK. If Andrew is indeed from the UK but posts on sites that end in any other top level domains (TLD), this search won't return hits from those sites.

Getting Lots of Results

In some cases you'd be interested in getting a lot of results, not just specific results. For instance, you want to find all Web sites or email addresses within a certain TLD. Here you want to combine your searches with keywords that do two things: get past the 1000 result restriction and increase your yield per search. As an example, consider finding Web sites in the ****.*gov* domain, as shown in Figure 5.5.

You will get a maximum of 1000 sites from the query, because it is most likely that you will get more than one result from a single site. In other words, if 500 pages are located on one server and 500 pages are located on another server you will only get two site results.

Also, you will be getting results from sites that are not within the ****.*gov* domain. How do we get more results and limit our search to the ****.*gov* domain? By combining the query with keywords and other operators. Consider the query *site:****.gov - www.****.gov*. The query means find any result within sites that are located in the ****.*gov* domain, but that are not on their main Web site. While this query works beautifully, it will again only get a maximum of 1000 results. There are some general additional keywords we can

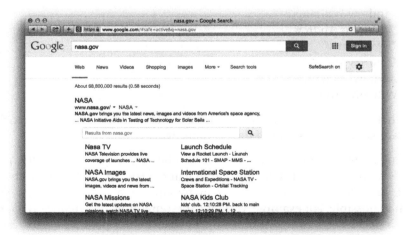

FIGURE 5.5

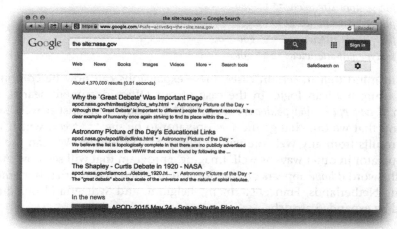

FIGURE 5.6

add to each query. The idea here is that we use words that will raise sites that were below the 1000 mark surface to within the first 1000 results. Although there is no guarantee that it will lift the other sites out, you could consider adding terms like *about*, *official*, *page*, *site*, and so on. While Google says that words like *the*, *a*, *or*, and so on are ignored during searches, we do see that results differ when combining these words with the *site:* operator. Looking at these results in Figure 5.6 shows that Google is indeed honoring the "ignored" words in our query.

More Combinations

When the idea is to find lots of results, you might want to combine your search with terms that will yield better results. For example, when looking for email addresses, you can add keywords like *contact*, *mail*, *email*, and *send*. When looking for telephone numbers you might use additional keywords like *phone*, *telephone*, *contact*, *number*, and *mobile*.

USING "SPECIAL" OPERATORS

Depending on what it is that we want to get from Google, we might have to use some of the other operators. Imagine we want to see what Microsoft Office documents are located on a Web site. We know we can use the *filetype:* operator to specify a certain file type, but we can only specify one type per query. As a result, we will need to automate the process of asking for each Office file type at a time. Consider asking Google these questions:

- *filetype:ppt site:www.****.gov*
- *filetype:doc site:www.****.gov*
- *filetype:xls site:www.****.gov*
- *filetype:pdf site:www.****.gov*

Keep in mind that in certain cases, these expansions can now be combined again using boolean logic. In the case of our Office document search, the search *filetype:ppt* or *filetype:doc site www.****.gov* could work just as well. Keep in mind that we can change the *site:* operator to be *site:****.gov*, which will fetch results from any Web site within the *****.gov* domain. We can use the *site:* operator in other ways as well. Imagine a program that will see how many time the word *iPhone* appears on sites located in different countries. If we monitor the Netherlands, France, Germany, Belgium, and Switzerland our query would be expanded as such:

- *iphone site:nl*
- *iphone site:fr*
- *iphone site:de*
- *iphone site:be*
- *iphone site:ch*

At this stage we only need to parse the returned page from Google to get the amount of results, and monitor how the iPhone campaign is/was spreading through Western Europe over time. Doing this right now (at the time of writing this book) would probably not give you meaningful results (as the hype has already peaked), but having this monitoring system in place before the release of the actual phone could have been useful. (For a list of all country codes see http://ftp.ics.uci.edu/pub/websoft/wwwstat/country-codes.txt, or just Google for Internet country codes.)

GETTING THE DATA FROM THE SOURCE

At the lowest level we need to make a Transmission Control Protocol (TCP) connection to our data source (which is the Google Web site) and ask for the results. Because Google is a Web application, we will connect to port 80. Ordinarily, we would use a Web browser, but if we are interested in automating the process we will need to be able to speak programmatically to Google.

SCRAPING IT YOURSELF: REQUESTING AND RECEIVING RESPONSES

This is the most flexible way to get results. You are in total control of the process and can do things like set the number of results (which was never possible with the Application Programming Interface (API)). But it is also the most labor intensive. However, once you get it going, your worries are over and you can start to tweak the parameters.

Scraping is not allowed by most Web applications.

To start we need to find out how to ask a question/query to the Web site. If you normally Google for something (in this case the word *test*), the returned Uniform Resource Locator (URL) looks like this:

http://www.google.co.za/search?hl=en&q=test&btnG=Search&meta=

The interesting bit sits after the first slash (/) – *search?hl=en&q=test&btnG= Search&meta=*. This is a GET request and parameters and their values are separated with an "&" sign. In this request we have passed four parameters:

- *hl*
- *q*
- *btnG*
- *meta*

The values for these parameters are separated from the parameters with the equal sign (=). The "*hl*" parameter means "home language," which is set to English. The "*q*" parameter means "question" or "query," which is set to our query "test." The other two parameters are not of importance (at least not now). Our search will return 10 results. If we set our preferences to return 100 results we get the following GET request: *http://www.google.co.za/search?num=1 00&hl=en&q=test&btnG=Search&meta=*. Note the additional parameter that is passed; "*num*" is set to 100. If we request the second page of results (e.g., results 101–200), the request looks as follows: *http://www.google.co.za/search?q=test&nu m=100&hl=en&start=100&sa=N*. There are a couple of things to notice here. The order in which the parameters are passed is ignored and yet the "*start*" parameter is added. The *start* parameter tells Google on which page we want to start getting results and the "*num*" parameter tell them how many results we want. Thus, following this logic, in order to get 301–400 results our request should look like this: *http://www.google.co.za/search?q=test&num=100&hl=en&start=300 &sa=N*. Let's try that and see what we get.

It seems to be working. Let's see what happens when we search for something a little more complex. The search *"testing testing 123" site:uk* results in the following query: *http://www.google.co.za/search?num=100&hl=en&q=%22testing+tes ting+123%22+site%3Auk&btnG=Search&meta=*

What happened there? Let's analyze it a bit. The *num* parameter is set to 100. The *btnG* and *meta* parameters can be ignored. The *site:* operator does not result in an extra parameter, but rather is located within the question or query. The question says *%22testing + testing + 123%22 + site%3Auk*. Actually, although the question seems a bit intimidating at first, there is really no magic there. The %22 is simply the hexadecimal encoded form of a quote ("). The %3A is the encoded form of a colon (:). Once we have replaced the encoded characters with their unencoded form, we have our original query back: *"testing testing 123" site:uk.*

So, how do you decide when to encode a character and when to use the unencoded form? This is a topic on it's own, but as a rule of thumb you cannot go wrong to encode everything that's not in the range A–Z, a–z, and 0–9. The encoding can be done programmatically, but if you are curious you can see all the encoded characters by typing man ascii in a UNIX terminal, by Googling for ascii hex encoding, or by visiting http://en.wikipedia.org/wiki/ASCII.

Now that we know how to formulate our request, we are ready to send it to Google and get a reply back. Note that the server will reply in Hypertext Markup Language (HTML). In it's simplest form, we can Telnet directly to Google's Web server and send the request by hand. Figure 5.7 shows how it is done.

The resultant HTML is truncated for brevity. In Figure 5.7, the commands that were typed out are highlighted. There are a couple of things to notice. The first is that we need to connect (Telnet) to the Web site on port 80 and wait for a connection before issuing our Hypertext Transfer Protocol (HTTP) request. The second is that our request is a GET that is followed by *"HTTP/1.0"* stating that we are speaking HTTP version 1.0 (you could also decide to speak 1.1). The last thing to notice is that we added the Host header, and ended our request with two carriage return line feeds (by pressing **Enter** two times). The server replied with a HTTP header (the part up to the two carriage return line feeds) and a body that contains the actual HTML (the bit that starts with *<html>*).

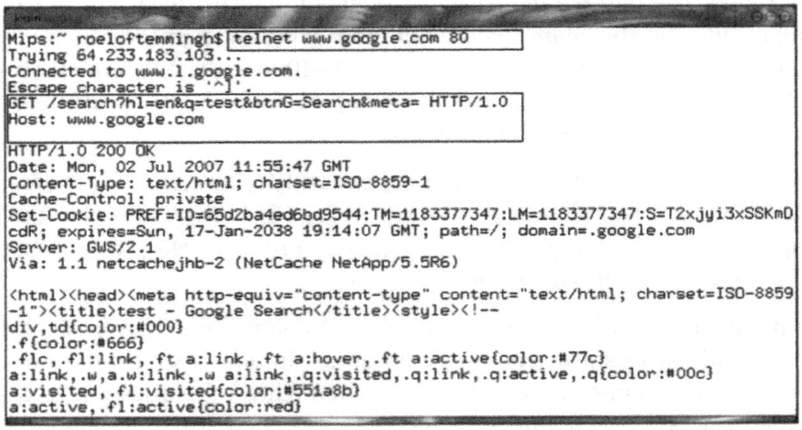

```
Mips:~ roeloftemmingh$ telnet www.google.com 80
Trying 64.233.183.103...
Connected to www.l.google.com.
Escape character is '^]'.
GET /search?hl=en&q=test&btnG=Search&meta= HTTP/1.0
Host: www.google.com

HTTP/1.0 200 OK
Date: Mon, 02 Jul 2007 11:55:47 GMT
Content-Type: text/html; charset=ISO-8859-1
Cache-Control: private
Set-Cookie: PREF=ID=65d2ba4ed6bd9544:TM=1183377347:LM=1183377347:S=T2xjyi3xSSKmD
cdR; expires=Sun, 17-Jan-2038 19:14:07 GMT; path=/; domain=.google.com
Server: GWS/2.1
Via: 1.1 netcachejhb-2 (NetCache NetApp/5.5R6)

<html><head><meta http-equiv="content-type" content="text/html; charset=ISO-8859
-1"><title>test - Google Search</title><style><!--
div,td{color:#000}
.f{color:#666}
.flc,.fl:link,.ft a:link,.ft a:hover,.ft a:active{color:#77c}
a:link,.w,a.w:link,.w a:link,.q:visited,.q:link,.q:active,.q{color:#00c}
a:visited,.fl:visited{color:#551a8b}
a:active,.fl:active{color:red}
```

FIGURE 5.7

This seems like a lot of work, but now that we know what the request looks like, we can start building automation around it. Let's try this with Netcat.

Netcat has been described as the Swiss Army Knife of TCP/Internet Protocol (IP). It is a tool that is used for good and evil; from catching the reverse shell from an exploit (evil) to helping network administrators dissect a protocol (good). In this case we will use it to send a request to Google's Web servers and show the resulting HTML on the screen. You can get Netcat for UNIX as well as Microsoft Windows by Googling "netcat download."

To describe the various switches and uses of Netcat is well beyond the scope of this chapter; therefore, we will just use Netcat to send the request to Google and catch the response. Before bringing Netcat into the equation, consider the following commands and their output:

```
$ echo "GET / HTTP/1.0";echo "Host: www.google.com"; echo

GET / HTTP/1.0

Host: www.google.com
```

Note that the last echo command (the blank one) adds the necessary carriage return line feed (CRLF) at the end of the HTTP request. To hook this up to Netcat and make it connect to Google's site we do the following:

```
$ (echo "GET / HTTP/1.0";echo "Host: www.google.com"; echo) | nc www.google.com
80
```

The output of the command is as follows:

```
HTTP/1.0 302 Found

Date: Mon, 02 Jul 2007 12:56:55 GMT

Content-Length: 221

Content-Type: text/html
```

The rest of the output is truncated for brevity. Note that we have parenthesis () around the echo commands, and the pipe character (|) that hooks it up to Netcat. Netcat makes the connection to www.google.com on port 80 and sends the output of the command to the left of the pipe character to the server. This particular way of hooking Netcat and echo together works on UNIX, but needs some tweaking to get it working under Windows.

There are other (easier) ways to get the same results. Consider the *"wget"* command (a Windows version of wget is available at http://xoomer.alice.it/hherold/). *Wget* in itself is a great tool, and using it only for sending requests to a Web server is a bit like contracting a rocket scientist to fix your microwave oven. To see all the other things *wget* can do, simply type *wget -h*. If we want to use *wget* to get the results of a query we can use it as follows:

wget http://www.google.co.za/search?hl=en&q=test-O output

The output looks like this:

--15:41:43-- http://www.google.com/search?hl=en&q=test

   => `output'

Resolving www.google.com... 64.233.183.103, 64.233.183.104, 64.233.183.147, ...

Connecting to www.google.com|64.233.183.103|:80... connected.

HTTP request sent, awaiting response... 403 Forbidden

15:41:44 ERROR 403: Forbidden.

The output of this command is the first indication that Google is not too keen on automated processes. What went wrong here? HTTP requests have a field called *"User-Agent"* in the header. This field is populated by applications that request Web pages (typically browsers, but also "grabbers" like *wget*), and is used to identify the browser or program. The HTTP header that *wget* generates looks like this:

GET /search?hl=en&q=test HTTP/1.0

User-Agent: Wget/1.10.1

*Accept: */**

Host: www.google.com

Connection: Keep-Alive

You can see that the *User-Agent* is populated with *Wget/1.10.1*. And that's the problem. Google inspects this field in the header and decides that you are using a tool that can be used for automation. Google does not like automating search queries and returns HTTP error code 403, Forbidden. Luckily this is not the end of the world. Because *wget* is a flexible program, you can set how it should report itself in the *User Agent* field. So, all we need to do is tell *wget* to report itself as something different than *wget*. This is done easily with an additional switch. Let's see what the header looks like when we tell *wget* to report itself as *"my_diesel_driven_browser."* We issue the command as follows:

$ wget -U my_diesel_drive_browser "http://www.google.com/search?hl=en&q=test" -O

output

The resultant HTTP request header looks like this:

GET /search?hl=en&q=test HTTP/1.0

User-Agent: my_diesel_drive_browser

*Accept: */**

Host: www.google.com

Connection: Keep-Alive

Note the changed *User-Agent.* Now the output of the command looks like this:

--15:48:55-- http://www.google.com/search?hl=en&q=test

    => `output'

Resolving www.google.com... 64.233.183.147, 64.233.183.99, 64.233.183.103, ...

Connecting to www.google.com|64.233.183.147|:80... connected.

HTTP request sent, awaiting response... 200 OK

Length: unspecified [text/html]

  [<=>   ] 17,913   37.65K/s

15:48:56 (37.63 KB/s) - `output' saved [17913]

The HTML for the query is located in the file called *"output"*. This example illustrates a very important concept – changing the *User-Agent*. Google has a large list of User-Agents that are not allowed.

Another popular program for automating Web requests is called *"curl,"* which is available for Windows at http://fileforum.betanews.com/detail/cURL_for_Windows/966899018/1. For Secure Sockets Layer (SSL) use, you may need to obtain the file *libssl32.dll* from somewhere else. Google for *libssl32.dll download.* Keep the EXE and the DLL in the same directory. As with *wget*, you will need to set the *User-Agent* to be able to use it. The default behavior of *curl* is to return the HTML from the query straight to standard output. The following is an example of using *curl* with an alternative *User-Agent* to return the HTML from a simple query. The command is as follows:

$ curl -A zoemzoemspecial "http://www.google.com/search?hl=en&q=test"

The output of the command is the raw HTML response. Note the changed *User-Agent*.

Google also uses the user agent of the Lynx text-based browser, which tries to render the HTML, leaving you without having to struggle through the HTML. This is useful for quick hacks like getting the amount of results for a query. Consider the following command:

$ lynx -dump "http://www.google.com/search?q=google" | grep Results | awk -F "of

about" '{print $2}' | awk '{print $1}'

1,020,000,000

Clearly, using UNIX commands like *sed*, *grep*, *awk*, and so on makes using Lynx with the dump parameter a logical choice in tight spots.

There are many other command line tools that can be used to make requests to Web servers. It is beyond the scope of this chapter to list all of the different tools. In most cases, you will need to change the *User-Agent* to be able to speak to Google. You can also use your favorite programming language to build the request yourself and connect to Google using sockets.

SCRAPING IT YOURSELF: THE BUTCHER SHOP

In the previous section, we learned how to Google a question and how to get HTML back from the server. While this is mildly interesting, it's not really that useful if we only end up with a heap of HTML. In order to make sense of the HTML, we need to be able to get individual results. In any scraping effort, this is the messy part of the mission. The first step of parsing results is to see if there is a structure to the results coming back. If there is a structure, we can unpack the data from the structure into individual results.

The FireBug extension from FireFox (https://addons.mozilla.org/firefox/downloads/latest/1843/addon-1843-latest.xpi?src=ss) can be used to easily map

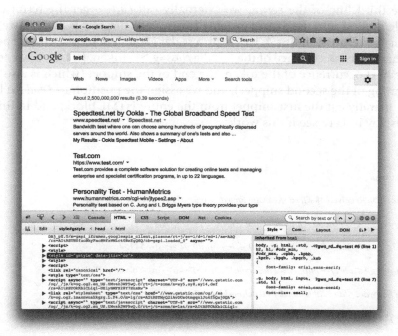

FIGURE 5.8

HTML code to visual structures. Viewing a Google results page in FireFox and inspecting a part of the results in FireBug looks like Figure 5.8.

With FireBug, every result snippet starts with the HTML code *<div class="g">*. With this in mind, we can start with a very simple PERL script that will only extract the first of the snippets. Consider the following code:

```
1 #!/bin/perl

2 use strict;

3 my $result=`curl -A moo "http://www.google.co.za/search?q=test&hl=en"`;

4 my $start=index($result,"<div class=g>");

5 my $end=index($result,"<div class=g",$start+1);

6 my $snippet=substr($result,$start,$end-$start);

7 print "\n\n".$snippet."\n\n";
```

In the third line of the script, we externally call *curl* to get the result of a simple request into the *$result* variable (the question/query is *test* and we get the first 10 results). In line 4, we create a scalar (*$start*) that contains the position of the first occurrence of the " < *div class=g* > " token. In Line 5, we look at the next occurrence of the token, the end of the snippet (which is also the beginning of the second snippet), and we assign the position to *$end*. In line 6, we literally cut the first snippet from the entire HTML block, and in line 7 we display it. Let's see if this works:

```
$ perl easy.pl

 % Total   % Received % Xferd  Average Speed  Time   Time    Time Current
                              Dload  Upload  Total  Spent  Left Speed
100 14367   0 14367   0    0  13141     0 --:--:-- 0:00:01 --:--:-- 54754
<div class=g><a href="http://www.test.com/" class=l><b>Test</b>.com Web Based
Testing Software</a><table border=0 cellpadding=0 cellspacing=0><tr><td
class="j"><font size=-1>Provides extranet privacy to clients making a range of
<b>tests</b> and surveys available to their human resources departments. Companies
can <b>test</b> prospective and <b>...</b><br><span
class=a>www.<b>test</b>.com/ -
28k - </span><nobr><a class=fl
href="http://64.233.183.104/search?q=cache:S9XHtkEncW8J:www.test.com/+test&hl=e
n&ct
=clnk&cd=1&gl=za&ie=UTF-8">Cached</a> - <a class=fl
href="/search?hl=en&ie=UTF-
8&q=related:www.test.com/">Similar
pages</a></nobr></font></td></tr></table></div>
```

It looks right when we compare it to what the browser says. The script now needs to somehow work through the entire HTML and extract all of the snippets. Consider the following PERL script:

```
1 #!/bin/perl

2 use strict;

3 my $result=`curl -A moo "http://www.google.com/search?q=test&hl=en"`;

4

5 my $start;

6 my $end;

7 my $token="<div class=g>";

8

9  while (1){

10  $start=index($result,$token,$start);

11  $end=index($result,$token,$start+1);

12  if ($start == -1 || $end == -1 || $start == $end){

13    last;

14  }

15

16  my $snippet=substr($result,$start,$end-$start);

17  print "\n-----\n".$snippet."\n----\n";

18  $start=$end;

19 }
```

While this script is a little more complex, it's still really simple. In this script we've put the "*<div class=g>*" string into a token, because we are going to use it more than once. This also makes it easy to change when Google decides to call it something else. In lines 9 through 19, a loop is constructed that will continue to look for the existence of the token until it is not found anymore. If it does not find a token (line 12), then the loop simply exists. In line 18, we move the position from where we are starting our search (for the token) to the position where we ended up in our previous search.

Running this script results in the different HTML snippets being sent to standard output. But this is only so useful. What we really want is to extract the URL, the title, and the summary from the snippet. For this we need a function that will accept four parameters: a string that contains a starting token, a string that contains the ending token, a scalar that will say where to search from, and a string that contains the HTML that we want to search within. We want this function to return the section that was extracted, as well as the new position where we are within the passed string. Such a function looks like this:

```
1 sub cutter{

2     my ($starttok,$endtok,$where,$str)=@_;

3      my $startcut=index($str,$starttok,$where)+length($starttok);

4     my $endcut=index($str,$endtok,$startcut+1);

5     my $returner=substr($str,$startcut,$endcut-$startcut);

6     my @res;

7     push @res,$endcut;

8    push @res,$returner;

9    return @res;

10 }
```

Now that we have this function, we can inspect the HTML and decide how to extract the URL, the summary, and the title from each snippet. The code to do this needs to be located within the main loop and looks as follows:

```
1 my ($pos,$url) = cutter("<a href=\"","\"",0,$snippet);

2 my ($pos,$heading) = cutter(">","</a>",$pos,$snippet);

3 my ($pos,$summary) = cutter("<font size=-1>","<br>",$pos,$snippet);
```

Notice how the URL is the first thing we encounter in the snippet. The URL itself is a hyperlink and always start with "<a href= and ends with a quote. Next up is the heading, which is within the hyperlink and as such starts with a ">" and ends with "</a>". Finally, it appears that the summary is always in a "<font size=-1>" and ends in a "<br>". Putting it all together we get the following PERL script:

```
#!/bin/perl

use strict;

my $result=`curl -A moo "http://www.google.com/search?q=test&hl=en"`;

my $start;

my $end;
```

```
my $token="<div class=g>";

while (1){

 $start=index($result,$token,$start);

 $end=index($result,$token,$start+1);

 if ($start == -1 || $end == -1 || $start == $end){

last; }

 my $snippet=substr($result,$start,$end-$start);

 my ($pos,$url) = cutter("<a href=\"","\"",0,$snippet);

 my ($pos,$heading) = cutter(">","</a>",$pos,$snippet);

 my ($pos,$summary) = cutter("<font size=-1>","<br>",$pos,$snippet);

 # remove <b> and </b>

 $heading=cleanB($heading);

 $url=cleanB($url);

 $summary=cleanB($summary);

 print "--->\nURL: $url\nHeading: $heading\nSummary:$summary\n<---\n\n";

 $start=$end;

}
```

Now that we have this function, we can inspect the HTML and decide how to extract the URL, the summary, and the title from each snippet. The code to do this needs to be located within the main loop and looks as follows:

```
1  my ($pos,$url) = cutter("<a href=\"","\"",0,$snippet);

2  my ($pos,$heading) = cutter(">","</a>",$pos,$snippet);

3  my ($pos,$summary) = cutter("<font size=-1>","<br>",$pos,$snippet);
```

Notice how the URL is the first thing we encounter in the snippet. The URL itself is a hyperlink and always start with "*<a href=* and ends with a quote. Next up is the heading, which is within the hyperlink and as such starts with a "*>*" and ends with "*</a>*". Finally, it appears that the summary is always in a "*<font size=-1>*" and ends in a "*
*". Putting it all together we get the following PERL script:

```perl
#!/bin/perl
use strict;
my $result=`curl -A moo "http://www.google.com/search?q=test&hl=en"`;
my $start;
my $end;
my $token="<div class=g>";
while (1){
  $start=index($result,$token,$start);
  $end=index($result,$token,$start+1);
  if ($start == -1 || $end == -1 || $start == $end){
last; }
  my $snippet=substr($result,$start,$end-$start);
  my ($pos,$url) = cutter("<a href=\"","\"",0,$snippet);
  my ($pos,$heading) = cutter(">","</a>",$pos,$snippet);
  my ($pos,$summary) = cutter("<font size=-1>","<br>",$pos,$snippet);
  # remove <b> and </b>
  $heading=cleanB($heading);
  $url=cleanB($url);
  $summary=cleanB($summary);
  print "--->\nURL: $url\nHeading: $heading\nSummary:$summary\n<---\n\n";
  $start=$end;
}
sub cutter{
  my ($starttok,$endtok,$where,$str)=@_;
  my $startcut=index($str,$starttok,$where)+length($starttok);
  my $endcut=index($str,$endtok,$startcut+1);
  my $returner=substr($str,$startcut,$endcut-$startcut);
  my @res;
  push @res,$endcut;
```

```
push @res,$returner;

return @res;

}

sub cleanB{

my ($str)=@_;

$str=~s/<b>//g;

$str=~s/<Vb>//g;

return $str;

}
```

Note that Google highlights the search term in the results. We therefore take the "and" tags out of the results, which is done in the *"cleanB"* subroutine. Let's see how this script works (see Figure 5.9).

It seems to be working. There could well be better ways of doing this with tweaking and optimization, but for a first pass it's not bad.

```
--->
URL: http://www.test.com/
Heading: Test.com Web Based Testing Software
Summary:Provides extranet privacy to clients making a range of tests and surveys
available to their human resources departments. Companies can test prospective an
d ...
<---

--->
URL: http://www.bandwidthplace.com/speedtest/
Heading: Bandwidth Speed Test
Summary:Personal Test. Test the speed of your Internet connection Free up to 3 ti
mes a month Purchase a subscription for. Up to 1000 tests per month; Personal tes
t ...
<---

--->
URL: http://www.nerdtests.com/ft_nq.php
Heading: NerdTests.com Fun Tests - Nerd Quiz
Summary:Determine your Nerd Quotient (NQ)! Quiz Brought to you by NerdTests.com.
<---

--->
URL: http://www.humanmetrics.com/cgi-win/JTypes2.asp
Heading: Online test based on Jung - Myers-Briggs typology
Summary:Online test based on Jung-Myers-Briggs personality approach provides your
 type formula, type description, and career choices.
<---

--->
URL: http://www.humanmetrics.com/cgi-win/JTypes1.htm
Heading: Personality test based on Jung - Myers-Briggs typology
Summary:Online test based on Jung-Myers-Briggs typology provides your personality
 formula, the description of your type, list of occupations, and option to assess
 ...
```

FIGURE 5.9

USING OTHER SEARCH ENGINES

Believe it or not, there are search engines other than Google! Bing search engine still supports an API and is worth looking into. But this book is not called Bing Hacking for Penetration Testers, so figuring out how to use the Bing API is left as an exercise for the reader.

PARSING THE DATA

Let's assume at this stage that everything is in place to connect to our data source (Google in this case), we are asking the right questions, and we have something that will give us results in neat plain text. For now, we are not going to worry how exactly that happens. It might be with a proxy API, scraping it yourself, or getting it from some provider. This section only deals with what you can do with the returned data.

To get into the right mindset, ask yourself what you as a human would do with the results. You may scan it for email addresses, Web sites, domains, telephone numbers, places, names, and surnames. As a human you are also able to put some context into the results. The idea here is that we put some of that human logic into a program. Again, computers are good at doing things over and over, without getting tired or bored, or demanding a raise. And as soon as we have the logic sorted out, we can add other interesting things like counting how many of each result we get, determining how much confidence we have in the results from a question, and how close the returned data is to the original question. But this is discussed in detail later on. For now let's concentrate on getting the basics right.

Parsing Email Addresses

There are many ways of parsing email addresses from plain text, and most of them rely on regular expressions. Regular expressions are like your quirky uncle that you'd rather not talk to, but the more you get to know him, the more interesting and cool he gets. If you are afraid of regular expressions you are not alone, but knowing a little bit about it can make your life a lot easier. If you are a regular expressions guru, you might be able to build a one-liner regex to effectively parse email addresses from plain text, but since I only know enough to make myself dangerous, we'll take it easy and only use basic examples. Let's look at how we can use it in a PERL program.

```
use strict;

my $to_parse="This is a test for roelof\@home.paterva.com - yeah right blah";

my @words;

#convert to lower case
```

```
$to_parse =~ tr/A-Z/a-z/;

#cut at word boundaries

push @words,split(/ /,$to_parse);

foreach my $word (@words){

  if ($word =~ /[a-z0-9._%+-]+@[a-z0-9.-]+\.[a-z]{2,4}/) {

    print $word."\n";

  }

}
```

This seems to work, but in the real world there are some problems. The script cuts the text into words based on spaces between words. But what if the text was *Is your address roelof@paterva.com?* Now the script fails. If we convert the @ sign, underscores (_), and dashes (-) to letter tokens, and then remove all symbols and convert the letter tokens back to their original values, it could work. Let's see:

```
use strict;

my $to_parse="Hey !! Is this a test for roelof-temmingh\@home.paterva.com? Right

!";

my @words;

print "Before: $to_parse\n";

#convert to lower case

$to_parse =~ tr/A-Z/a-z/;

#convert 'special' chars to tokens

$to_parse=convert_xtoX($to_parse);

#blot all symbols

$to_parse=~s/\W/ /g;

#convert back

$to_parse=convert_Xtox($to_parse);

print "After: $to_parse\n";
```

```perl
#cut at word boundaries
push @words,split(/ /,$to_parse);
print "\nParsed email addresses follows:\n";
foreach my $word (@words){
  if ($word =~ /[a-z0-9._%+-]+@[a-z0-9.-]+\.[a-z]{2,4}/) {
    print $word."\n";
} }
sub convert_xtoX {
  my ($work)=@_;
  $work =~ s/\@/AT/g;
  $work =~ s/_/UNSC/g;  $work =~ s/-/DASH/g;
  return $work;
}
sub convert_Xtox{
  my ($work)=@_;
  $work =~ s/AT/\@/g;   $work =~ s/DOT/\./g;
  $work =~ s/UNSC/_/g;  $work =~ s/DASH/-/g;
  return $work;
}
```

Right – let's see how this works.

$ perl parse-email-2.pl

Before: Hey !! Is this a test for roelof-temmingh@home.paterva.com? Right !

After: hey is this a test for roelof-temmingh@home.paterva.com right

Parsed email addresses follows:

roelof-temmingh@home.paterva.com

It seems to work, but still there are situations where this is going to fail. What if the line reads *"My email address is roelof@paterva.com."*? Notice the period after the email address. The parsed address is going to retain that period. Luckily that can be fixed with a simple replacement rule; changing a dot space sequence to two spaces. In PERL:

```
$to_parse =~ s/\. / /g;
```

With this in place, we now have something that will effectively parse 99% of valid email addresses (and about 5% of invalid addresses). Admittedly the script is not the most elegant, optimized, and pleasing, but it works!

Remember the expansions we did on email addresses in the previous section? We now need to do the exact opposite. In other words, if we find the text *"andrew at syngress.com"* we need to know that it's actually an email address. This has the disadvantage that we will create false positives. Think about a piece of text that says *"you can contact us at paterva.com."* If we convert *at* back to @, we'll parse an email that reads *us@paterva.com*. But perhaps the pros outweigh the cons, and as a general rule you'll catch more real email addresses than false ones. (This depends on the domain as well. If the domain belongs to a company that normally adds a *.com* to their name, for example *amazon.com*, chances are you'll get false positives before you get something meaningful). We furthermore want to catch addresses that include the *_remove_* or *removethis* tokens.

To do this in PERL is a breeze. We only need to add these translations in front of the parsing routines. Let's look at how this would be done:

```
sub expand_ats{

 my ($work)=@_;

$work=~s/remove//g;

 $work=~s/removethis//g;

 $work=~s/_remove_//g;

 $work=~s/\(remove\)//g;

 $work=~s/_removethis_//g;

 $work=~s/\s*(\@)\s*/\@/g;

 $work=~s/\s+at\s+/\@/g;

 $work=~s/\s*\(at\)\s*/\@/g;

 $work=~s/\s*\[at\]\s*/\@/g;

 $work=~s/\s*\.at\.\s*/\@/g;

 $work=~s/\s*_at_\s*/\@/g;
```

```
$work=~s/\s*\@\s*/\@/g;

$work=~s/\s*dot\s*/\./g;

$work=~s/\s*\[dot\]\s*/\./g;

$work=~s/\s*\(dot\)\s*/\./g;

$work=~s/\s*_dot_\s*/\./g;

$work=~s/\s*\.\s*/\./g;

return $work;

}
```

These replacements are bound to catch lots of email addresses, but could also be prone to false positives. Let's give it a run and see how it works with some test data:

```
$ perl parse-email-3.pl

Before: Testing test1 at paterva.com

This is normal text. For a dot matrix printer.

This is normal text...no really it is!

At work we all need to work hard

test2@paterva dot com

test3 _at_ paterva dot com

test4(remove) (at) paterva [dot] com

roelof @ paterva . com

I want to stay at home. Really I do.
```

After: testing *test1@paterva.com* this is normal text.for a.matrix printer.this is normal text...no really it is @work we all need to work hard test2@paterva.com test3@paterva.com test4@paterva.com roelof@paterva.com i want to stay@home.really i do.

```
Parsed email addresses follows:

test1@paterva.com

test2@paterva.com

test3@paterva.com

roelof@paterva.com

stay@home.really
```

For the test run, you can see that it caught four of the five test email addresses and included one false positive. Depending on the application, this rate of false positives might be acceptable because they are quickly spotted using visual inspection. Again, the 80/20 principle applies here; with 20% effort you will catch 80% of email addresses. If you are willing to do some postprocessing, you might want to check if the email addresses you've mined ends in any of the known TLDs (see next section). But, as a rule, if you want to catch all email addresses (in all of the obscured formats), you can be sure to either spend a lot of effort or deal with plenty of false positives.

DOMAINS AND SUBDOMAINS

Luckily, domains and subdomains are easier to parse if you are willing to make some assumptions. What is the difference between a hostname and a domain name? How do you tell the two apart? Seems like a silly question. Clearly *www.paterva.com* is a hostname and *paterva.com* is a domain, because *www.paterva.com* has an IP address and *paterva.com* does not. But the domain *google.com* (and many others) resolve to an IP address as well. Then again, you know that *google.com* is a domain. What if we get a Google hit from *fpd.gsfc.****.gov*? Is it a hostname or a domain? Or a CNAME for something else? Instinctively you would add *www.* to the name and see if it resolves to an IP address. If it does then it's a domain. But what if there is no *www* entry in the zone? Then what's the answer?

A domain needs a name server entry in its zone. A hostname does not have to have a name server entry, in fact it very seldom does. If we make this assumption, we can make the distinction between a domain and a host. The rest seems easy. We simply cut our Google URL field into pieces at the dots and put it back together. Let's take the site *fpd.gsfc.****.gov* as an example. The first thing we do is figure out if it's a domain or a site by checking for a name server. It does not have a name server, so we can safely ignore the *fpd* part, and end up with *gsfc.****.gov*. From there we get the domains:

- *gsfc.****.gov****.gov*
- *gov*

There is one more thing we'd like to do. Typically we are not interested in TLDs or even sub-TLDs. If you want to you can easily filter these out. There is another interesting thing we can do when looking for domains. We can recursively call our script with any new information that we've found. The input for our domain hunting script is typically going to be a domain, right? If we feed the domain *****.gov* to our script, we are limited to 1000 results. If our script digs up the domain *gsfc.****.gov*, we can now feed it back into the same script, allowing for 1000 fresh results on this subdomain (which might give us deeper subdomains). Finally, we can have our script terminate when no new subdomains are found.

Another way of obtaining domains without having to perform the host/domain check is to post process-mined email addresses. As almost all email addresses are already at a domain (and not a host), the email address can simply be cut after the @ sign and used in a similar fashion.

TELEPHONE NUMBERS

Telephone numbers are very hard to parse with an acceptable rate of false positives (unless you limit it to a specific country). This is because there is no standard way of writing down a telephone number. Some people add the country code, but on regional sites (or mailing lists) it's seldom done. And even if the country code is added, it could be added by using a plus sign (e.g., +44) or using the local international dialing method (e.g., 0044). It gets worse. In most cases, if the city code starts with a zero, it is omitted if the internal dialing code is added (e.g., +27 12 555 1234 vs. 012 555 1234). And then some people put the zero in parentheses to show it's not needed when dialing from abroad (e.g., +27 (0)12 555 1234). To make matters worse, a lot of European nations like to split the last four digits in groups of two (e.g., 012 12 555 12 34). Of course, there are those people that remember numbers in certain patterns, thereby breaking all formats and making it almost impossible to determine which part is the country code (if at all), the city, and the area within the city (e.g., +271 25 551 234).

Then as an added bonus, dates can look a lot like telephone numbers. Consider the text "*From 1823-1825 1520 people couldn't parse telephone numbers.*" Better still are time frames such as "*Andrew Williams: 1971-04-01 – 2007-07-07.*" And, while it's not that difficult for a human to spot a false positive when dealing with email addresses, you need to be a local to tell the telephone number of a plumber in Burundi from the ISBN number of "Stealing the network." So, is all lost? Not quite. There are two solutions: the hard but cheap solution and the easy but costly solution. In the hard but cheap solution, we will apply all of the logic we can think of to telephone numbers and live with the false positives. In the easy (OK, it's not even that easy) solution, we'll buy a list of country, city, and regional codes from a provider. Let's look at the hard solution first.

One of the most powerful principles of automation is that if you can figure out how to do something as a human being, you can code it. It is when you cannot write down what you are doing when automation fails. If we can code all the things we know about telephone numbers into an algorithm, we have a shot at getting it right. The following are some of the important rules that I have used to determine if something is a real telephone number.

- Convert *00* to +, but only if the number starts with it.
- Remove instances of *(0)*.
- Length must be between 9 and 13 numbers.
- Has to contain at least one space (optional for low tolerance).
- Cannot contain two (or more) single digits (e.g., 2383 5 3 231 will be thrown out).

- Should not look like a date (various formats).
- Cannot have a plus sign if it's not at the beginning of the number.
- Less than four numbers before the first space (unless it starts with a + or a *0*).
- Should not have the string "ISBN" in near proximity.
- Rework the number from the last number to the first number and put it in *+XX- XXX-XXX-XXXX* format.

To find numbers that need to comply to these rules is not easy. I ended up not using regular expressions but rather a nested loop, which counts the number of digits and accepted symbols (pluses, dashes, and spaces) in a sequence. Once it's reached a certain number of acceptable characters followed by a number of unacceptable symbols, the result is sent to the verifier (that use the rules listed above). If verified, it is repackaged to try to get in the right format. Of course this method does not always work. In fact, approximately one in five numbers are false positives. But the technique seldom fails to spot a real telephone number, and more importantly, it does not cost anything. There are better ways to do this. If we have a list of all country and city codes we should be able to figure out the format as well as verify if a sequence of numbers is indeed a telephone number. Such a list exists but is not in the public domain.

Because I don't have the complete database, I don't have code for this, but suspect that you will need to write a program that will measure the distance between the first couple of numbers from the parsed number to those in the list. You will surely end up in a situation where there is more than one possibility. This will happen because the same number might exist in multiple countries and if they are specified on the Web page without a country code it's impossible to determine in which country they are located.

The database can be bought at www.numberingplans.com, but they are rather strict about selling the database to just anyone. They also provide a nifty lookup interface (limited to just a couple of lookups a day), which is not just for phone numbers. But that's a story for another day.

POSTPROCESSING

Even when we get good data back from our data source there might be the need to do some form of postprocessing on it. Perhaps you want to count how many of each result you mined in order to sort it by frequency. In the next section we look at some things that you should consider doing.

Sorting Results by Relevance

If we parse an email address when we search for "Andrew Williams," that email address would almost certainly be more interesting than the email addresses we would get when searching for "A Williams." Indeed, some of the expansions we've done in the previous section borders on desperation. Thus, what we need is a method of implementing a "confidence" to a search. This is actually not that difficult. Simply assign this confidence index to every result you parse.

There are other ways of getting the most relevant result to bubble to the top of a result list. Another way is simply to look at the frequency of a result. If you parse the email address *andrew@syngress.com* ten times more than any other email address, the chances are that that email address is more relevant than an email address that only appears twice.

Yet another way is to look at how the result correlates back to the original search term. The result *andrew@syngress.com* looks a lot like the email address for Andrew Williams. It is not difficult to write an algorithm for this type of correlation. An example of such a correlation routine looks like this:

```
sub correlate{
  my ($org,$test)=@_;
  print " [$org] to [$test] : ";
  my $tester;  my $beingtest;
  my $multi=1;
#determine which is the longer string
if (length($org) > length($test)){
  $tester=$org;   $beingtest=$test;
} else {
  $tester=$test;   $beingtest=$org;
}
#loop for every 3 letters
for (my $index=0; $index<=length($tester)-3; $index++){
  my $threeletters=substr($tester,$index,3);
  if ($beingtest =~ /$threeletters/i){
    $multi=$multi*2;
  }
}
print "$multi\n";
return $multi;
}
```

This routine breaks the longer of the two strings into sections of three letters and compares these sections to the other (shorter) string. For every section that matches, the resultant return value is doubled. This is by no means a "standard" correlation function, but will do the trick, because basically all we need is something that will recognize parts of an email address as looking similar to the first name or the last name. Let's give it a quick spin and see how it works. Here we will "weigh" the results of the following email addresses to an original search of "Roelof Temmingh":

[Roelof Temmingh] to [roelof.temmingh@abc.co.za] : 8192

[Roelof Temmingh] to [rtemmingh@abc.co.za] : 64

[Roelof Temmingh] to [roeloft@abc.co.za] : 16

[Roelof Temmingh] to [TemmiRoe882@abc.co.za] : 16

[Roelof Temmingh] to [kosie@temmingh.org] : 64

[Roelof Temmingh] to [kosie.kramer@yahoo.com] : 1

[Roelof Temmingh] to [Tempest@yahoo.com] : 2

This seems to work, scoring the first address as the best, and the two addresses containing the entire last name as a distant second. What's interesting is to see that the algorithm does not know what is the username and what is a domain. This is something that you might want to change by simply cutting the email address at the @ sign and only comparing the first part. On the other hand, it might be interesting to see domains that look like the first name or last name.

There are two more ways of weighing a result. The first is by looking at the distance between the original search term and the parsed result on the resultant page. In other words, if the email address appears right next to the term that you searched for, the chances are more likely that it's more relevant than when the email address is 20 paragraphs away from the search term. The second is by looking at the importance (or popularity) of the site that gives the result. This means that results coming from a site that is more popular is more relevant than results coming from sites that only appear on page five of the Google results. Luckily by just looking at Google results, we can easily implement both of these requirements. A Google snippet only contains the text surrounding the term that we searched for, so we are guaranteed some proximity (unless the parsed result is separated from the parsed results by "..."). The importance or popularity of the site can be obtained by the Pagerank of the site. By assigning a value to the site based on the position in the results (e.g., if the site appears first in the results or only much later) we can get a fairly good approximation of the importance of the site.

A note of caution here. These different factors need to be carefully balanced. Things can go wrong quickly. Imagine that Andrew's email address is whipmaster@midgets.com, and that he always uses the alias *"WhipMaster"* when posting from this email address. As a start, our correlation to the original term (assuming we searched for *Andrew Williams*) is not going to result in a null value. And if the email address does not appear many times in different places, it will also throw the algorithm off the trail. As such, we may choose to only increase the index by 10% for every three-letter word that matches, as the code stands a 100% increase if used. But that's the nature of automation, and the reason why these types of tools ultimately assist but do not replace humans.

Beyond Snippets

There is another type of postprocessing we can do, but it involves lots of bandwidth and loads of processing power. If we expand our mining efforts to the actual page that is returned (i.e., not just the snippet) we might get many more results and be able to do some other interesting things. The idea here is to get the URL from the Google result, download the entire page, convert it to plain text (as best as we can), and perform our mining algorithms on the text. In some cases, this expansion would be worth the effort (imagine looking for email addresses and finding a page that contains a list of employees and their email addresses. What a gold mine!). It also allows for parsing words and phrases, something that has a lot less value when only looking at snippets.

Parsing and sorting words or phrases from entire pages is best left to the experts (think the PhDs at Google), but nobody says that we can't try our hand at some very elementary processing. As a start we will look at the frequency of words across all pages. We'll end up with common words right at the top (e.g., *the*, *and*, and *friends*). We can filter these words using one of the many lists that provides the top ten words in a specific language. The resultant text will give us a general idea of what words are common across all the pages; in other words, an idea of "what this is about." We can extend the words to phrases by simply concatenating words together. A next step would be looking at words or phrases that are not used in high frequency in a single page, but that has a high frequency when looking across many pages. In other words, what we are looking for are words that are only used once or twice in a document (or Web page), but that are used on all the different pages. The idea here is that these words or phrases will give specific information about the subject.

Presenting Results

As many of the searches will use expansion and thus result in multiple searches, with the scraping of many Google pages we'll need to finally consolidate all of the subresults into a single result. Typically this will be a list of results and we will need to sort the results by their relevance.

COLLECTING SEARCH TERMS

Google's ability to collect search terms is very powerful. If you doubt this, visit the Google ZeitGeist page. Google has the ability to know what's on the mind of just about everyone that's connected to the Internet. They can literally read the minds of the (online) human race.

If you know what people are looking for, you can provide them (i.e., sell to them) that information. In fact, you can create a crude economic model. The number of searches for a phrase is the "demand " while the number of pages containing the phrase is the "supply." The price of a piece of information is related to the demand divided by the supply. And while Google will probably (let's hope) never implement such billing, it would be interesting to see them adding this as some form of index on the results page.

Let's see what we can do to get some of that power. This section looks at ways of obtaining the search terms of other users.

Spying on Your Own

When you search for something, the query goes to Google's computers. Every time you do a search at Google, they check to see if you are passing along a cookie. If you are not, they instruct your browser to set a cookie. The browser will be instructed to pass along that cookie for every subsequent request to any Google system (e.g., *.google.com), and to keep doing it until 2038. Thus, two searches that were done from the same laptop in two different countries, two years apart, will both still send the same cookie (given that the cookie store was never cleared), and Google will know it's coming from the same user. The query has to travel over the network, so if I can get it as it travels to them, I can read it. This technique is called "sniffing." In the previous sections, we've seen how to make a request to Google. Let's see what a cookieless request looks like, and how Google sets the cookie:

```
$ telnet www.google.co.za 80

Trying 64.233.183.99...

Connected to www.google.com.

Escape character is '^]'.

GET / HTTP/1.0

Host: www.google.co.za

HTTP/1.0 200 OK

Date: Thu, 12 Jul 2007 08:20:24 GMT
```

Content-Type: text/html; charset=ISO-8859-1

Cache-Control: private

Set-Cookie:

PREF=ID=329773239358a7d2:TM=1184228424:LM=1184228424:S=MQ6vKrgT4f9u

p_gj;

expires=Sun, 17-Jan-2038 19:14:07 GMT; path=/; domain=.google.co.za

Server: GWS/2.1

Via: 1.1 netcachejhb-2 (NetCache NetApp/5.5R6)

<html><head>....snip...

Notice the *Set-Cookie* part. The ID part is interesting. The other cookies (*TM* and *LM*) contain the birth date of the cookie (in seconds from 1970), and when the preferences were last changed. The ID stays constant until you clear your cookie store in the browser. This means every subsequent request coming from your browser will contain the cookie.

If we have a way of reading the traffic to Google we can use the cookie to identify subsequent searches from the same browser. There are two ways to be able to see the requests going to Google. The first involves setting up a sniffer somewhere along the traffic, which will monitor requests going to Google. The second is a lot easier and involves infrastructure that is almost certainly already in place; using proxies. There are two ways that traffic can be proxied. The user can manually set a proxy in his or her browser, or it can be done transparently somewhere upstream. With a transparent proxy, the user is mostly unaware that the traffic is sent to a proxy, and it almost always happens without the user's consent or knowledge. Also, the user has no way to switch the proxy on or off. By default, all traffic going to port 80 is intercepted and sent to the proxy. In many of these installations other ports are also intercepted, typically standard proxy ports like 3128, 1080, and 8080. Thus, even if you set a proxy in your browser, the traffic is intercepted before it can reach the manually con-figured proxy and is sent to the transparent proxy. These transparent proxies are typically used at boundaries in a network, say at your ISP's Internet gateway or close to your company's Internet connection.

On the one hand, we have Google that is providing a nice mechanism to keep track of your search terms, and on the other hand we have these wonderful transparent devices that collect and log all of your traffic. Seems like a perfect combination for data mining.

Let's see how can we put something together that will do all of this for us. As a start we need to configure a proxy to log the entire request header and the GET parameters as well as accepting connections from a transparent network redirect. To do this you can use the popular Squid proxy with a mere three modifications to the stock standard configuration file. These three lines that you need are:

The first tells Squid to accept connections from the transparent redirect on port 3128:

http_port 3128 transparent

The second tells Squid to log the entire HTTP request header:

log_mime_hdrs on

The last line tells Squid to log the GET parameters, not just the host and path:

strip_query_terms off

With this set and the Squid proxy running, the only thing left to do is to send traffic to it. This can be done in a variety of ways and it is typically done at the firewall. Assuming you are running FreeBSD with all the kernel options set to support it (and the Squid proxy is on the same box), the following one liner will direct all outgoing traffic to port 80 into the Squid box:

ipfw add 10 fwd 127.0.0.1,3128 tcp from any to any 80

Similar configurations can be found for other operating systems and/or firewalls. Google for "transparent proxy network configuration" and choose the appropriate one. With this set we are ready to intercept all Web traffic that originates behind the firewall. While there is a lot of interesting information that can be captured from these types of Squid logs, we will focus on Google-related requests.

Once your transparent proxy is in place, you should see requests coming in. The following is a line from the proxy log after doing a simple search on the phrase "test phrase":

1184253638.293   752 196.xx.xx.xx TCP_MISS/200 4949 GET

http://www.google.co.za/search?hl=en&q=test+phrase&btnG=Google+Search&meta=

-

DIRECT/72.14.253.147 text/html [Host: www.google.co.za\r\nUser-Agent: Mozilla/5.0

(Macintosh; U; Intel Mac OS X; en-US; rv:1.8.1.4) Gecko/20070515

Firefox/2.0.0.4\r\nAccept:

text/xml,application/xml,application/xhtml+xml,text/html;q=0.9,text/plain;q=0.8,ima

ge/png,*/*;q=0.5\r\nAccept-Language: en-us,en;q=0.5\r\nAccept-Encoding:

gzip,deflate\r\nAccept-Charset: ISO-8859-1,utf-8;q=0.7,*;q=0.7\r\nKeep-Alive:

300\r\nProxy-Connection: keep-alive\r\nReferer: http://www.google.co.za/\r\nCookie:

PREF=ID=35d1cc1c7089ceba:TM=1184106010:LM=1184106010:S=gBAPGByiXrA7Z

PQN\r\n]

[HTTP/1.0 200 OK\r\nCache-Control: private\r\nContent-Type: text/html;

charset=UTF-

8\r\nServer: GWS/2.1\r\nContent-Encoding: gzip\r\nDate: Thu, 12 Jul 2007 09:22:01

GMT\r\nConnection: Close\r\n\r]

Notice the search term appearing as the value of the "*q*" parameter "*test + phrase.*" Also notice the ID cookie that is set to "*35d1cc1c7089ceba.*" This value of the cookie will remain the same regardless of subsequent search terms. In the text above, the IP number that made the request is also listed (but mostly crossed out). From here on it is just a question of implementation to build a system that will extract the search term, the IP address, and the cookie and shove it into a database for further analysis. A system like this will silently collect search terms day in and day out.

How to Spot a Transparent Proxy

In some cases it is useful to know if you are sitting behind a transparent proxy. There is a quick way of finding out. Telnet to port 80 on a couple of random IP addresses that are outside of your network. If you get a connection every time, you are behind a transparent proxy. (Note: try not to use private IP address ranges when conducting this test.)

Another way is looking up the address of a Web site, then Telnetting to the IP number, issuing a GET/HTTP/1.0 (without the Host: header), and looking at the response. Some proxies use the Host: header to determine where you want to connect, and without it should give you an error.

$ host www.paterva.com

www.paterva.com has address 64.71.152.104

$ telnet 64.71.152.104 80

Trying 64.71.152.104...

Connected to linode.

Escape character is '^]'.

GET / HTTP/1.0

HTTP/1.0 400 Bad Request

Server: squid/2.6.STABLE12

Not only do we know we are being transparently proxied, but we can also see the type and server of the proxy that's used. Note that the second method does not work with all proxies, especially the bigger proxies in use at many ISPs.

Referrals

Another way of finding out what people are searching for is to look at the *Referer:* header of requests coming to your Web site. Of course there are limitations. The idea here being that someone searches for something on Google, your site shows up on the list of results, and they click on the link that points to your site. While this might not be super exciting for those with none or low traffic sites, it works great for people with access to very popular sites. How does it actually work? Every site that you visit knows about the previous site that you visited. This is sent in the HTTP header as a referrer. When someone visits Google, their search terms appear as part of the URL (as it's a GET request) and are passed to your site once the user arrives there. This gives you the ability to see what they searched for before they got to your site, which is very useful for marketing people.

Typically an entry in an Apache log that came from a Google search looks like this:

68.144.162.191 - - [10/Jul/2007:11:45:25 -0400] "GET /evolution-gui.html HTTP/1.1"

304 - "http://www.google.com/search?hl=en&q=evolution+beta+gui&btnG=Search"

"Mozilla/5.0 (Windows; U; Windows NT 5.1; en-GB; rv:1.8.1.4) Gecko/20070515

Firefox/2.0.0.4"

From this entry we can see that the user was searching for *"evolution beta gui"* on Google before arriving at our page, and that he or she then ended up at the *"/evolution-gui.html"* page. A lot of applications that deal with analyzing Web logs have the ability to automatically extract these terms for your logs, and present you with a nice list of terms and their frequency.

Is there a way to use this to mine search terms at will? Not likely. The best option (and it's really not that practical) is to build a popular site with various types of content and see if you can attract visitors with the only reason to mine their search terms. Again, you'll surely have better uses for these visitors than just their search terms.

SUMMARY

In this chapter we looked at various ways that you can use Google to dig up useful information. The power of searching really comes to life when you have the ability to automate certain processes. This chapter showed how this automation might be achieved using simple scripts. Also, the fun really starts when you have the means of connecting bits of information together to form a complete picture (e.g., not just searching, but also performing additional functions with the mined information). The tools and tricks shown in the chapter is really only the top of a massive iceberg called *data collection* (or *mining*). Hopefully it will open your mind as to what can be achieved. The idea was never to completely exhaust every possible avenue in detail, but rather to get your mind going in the right direction and to stimulate creative thoughts. If the chapter has inspired you to hack together your own script to perform something amazing, it has served its purpose (and I would love to hear from you).

CHAPTER 6

Locating Exploits and Finding Targets

INTRODUCTION

Exploits are tools of the hacker trade. Designed to penetrate a target, most hackers have many different exploits at their disposal. Some exploits, termed *zero day* or *0day*, remain underground for some period of time, eventually becoming public, posted to newsgroups or Web sites for the world to share. With so many Web sites dedicated to the distribution of exploit code, it's fairly simple to harness the power of Google to locate these tools. It can be a slightly more difficult exercise to locate potential targets, even though many modern Web application security advisories include a Google search designed to locate potential targets.

In this chapter we'll explore methods of locating exploit code and potentially vulnerable targets. These are not strictly "dark side" exercises, since security professionals often use public exploit code during a vulnerability assessment. However, only blackhats use those tools against systems without prior consent.

LOCATING EXPLOIT CODE

Untold hundreds and thousands of Web sites are dedicated to providing exploits to the general public. Blackhats generally provide exploits to aid fellow blackhats in the hacking community. White hats provide exploits as a way of eliminating false positives from automated tools during an assessment. Simple searches such as *remote exploit* and *vulnerable exploit* locate exploit sites by focusing on common lingo used by the security community. Other searches, such as *inurl:0day*, don't work nearly as well as they used to, but old standbys like *inurl:sploits* still work fairly well. The problem is that most security folks don't just troll the Internet looking for exploit caches; most of them frequent a handful of sites for the more mainstream tools, venturing to a search engine only when their bookmarked sites fail them. When it comes to trolling the Web for a specific security tool, Google's a great place to turn up at first.

Locating Public Exploit Sites

One way to locate exploit code is to focus on the file extension of the source code and then search for specific content within that code. Since source code is the text-based representation of the difficult-to-read machine code, Google is well suited for this task. For example, a large number of exploits are written in C, which generally uses source code ending in a .c extension. Of course, a search for *filetype:c c* returns nearly 500,000 results, meaning that we need to narrow our search. A query for *filetype:c exploit* returns around 5,000 results, most of which are exactly the types of programs we're looking for. Bearing in mind that these are the most popular sites hosting C source code containing the word *exploit*, the returned list is a good start for a list of bookmarks. Using page-scraping techniques, we can isolate these sites by running a UNIX command such as:

grep Cached exploit_file | awk –F" –" '{print $1}' | sort –u

against the dumped Google results page. Using good, old-fashioned cut and paste or a command such as *lynx –dump* works well for capturing the page this way. The slightly polished results of scraping 20 results from Google in this way are shown in the list as follows.

download2.rapid7.com/r7-0025 securityvulns.com/files

www.outpost9.com/exploits/unsorted

downloads.securityfocus.com/vulnerabilities/exploits

packetstorm.linuxsecurity.com/0101-exploits

packetstorm.linuxsecurity.com/0501-exploits packetstormsecurity.nl/0304-

exploits www.packetstormsecurity.nl/0009-exploits www.0xdeadbeef.info

archives.neohapsis.com/archives/ packetstormsecurity.org/0311-exploits

packetstormsecurity.org/0010-exploits www.critical.lt

synnergy.net/downloads/exploits www.digitalmunition.com

www.safemode.org/files/zillion/exploits vdb.dragonsoft.com.tw

unsecure.altervista.org www.darkircop.org/security

www.w00w00.org/files/exploits/

LOCATING EXPLOITS VIA COMMON CODE STRINGS

Since Web pages display source code in various ways, a source code listing could have practically any file extension. A PHP page might generate a text view of a C file, for example, making the file extension from Google's perspective .PHP instead of .C.

Another way to locate exploit code is to focus on common strings within the source code itself. One way to do this is to focus on common inclusions or header file references. For example, many C programs include the standard input/output library functions, which are referenced by an *include* statement such as *#include <stdio.h>* within the source code. A query such as *"#include <stdio.h>"* exploit would locate C source code that contained the word *exploit*, regardless of the file's extension. This would catch code (and code fragments) that are displayed in HTML documents. Extending the search to include programs that include a friendly usage statement with a query such as *"#include <stdio.h>"* usage exploit returns the results shown in Figure 6.1.

This search returns quite a few hits, nearly all of which contain exploit code. Using traversal techniques (or simply hitting up the main page of the site) can reveal other exploits or tools. Notice that most of these hits are HTML documents, which our previous *filetype:c* query would have excluded. There are lots of ways to locate source code using common code strings, but not all source code can be fit into a nice, neat little box. Some code can be nailed down fairly neatly using this technique; other code might require a bit more query tweaking.

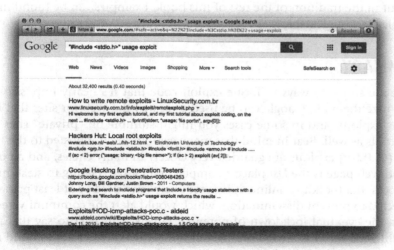

FIGURE 6.1

LOCATING VULNERABLE TARGETS

Attackers are increasingly using Google to locate Web-based targets vulnerable to specific exploits. In fact, it's not uncommon for public vulnerability announcements to contain Google links to potentially vulnerable targets.

Locating Targets via Vulnerability Disclosures

Software vendors and security researchers regularly post advisories about vulnerable software that display a link to the affected software vendor's Web site. Not all advisories list such a link, but a quick Google query should help you locate the vendor's page. Since our goal is to develop a query string to locate vulnerable targets on the Web, the vendor's Web site is a good place to discover what exactly the product's Web pages look like. Especially useful is the "Powered by ..." search string.

LOCATING TARGETS VIA SOURCE CODE

In some cases, a good query is not as easy to come by, although as we'll see, the resultant query is nearly identical in construction. Although this method is more drawn out (and could be short-circuited by creative thinking), it shows a typical process for detecting an exact working query for locating vulnerable targets. Here we take a look at how a hacker might use the source code of a program to discover ways to search for that software with Google. A phrase like "Powered by" can be very useful in locating specific targets due to their high degree of uniqueness.

Too many examples of this technique are in action to even begin to list them all, but in the tradition of the rest of this book, Examples can be found in the Google Hacking Database.

SUMMARY

There are so many ways to locate exploit code that it's nearly impossible to categorize them all. Google can be used to search the Web for sites that host public exploits, and in some cases you might stumble on "private" sites that host tools as well. Bear in mind that many exploits are not posted to the Web. New (or 0day) exploits are guarded very closely in many circles, and an open public Web page is the *last* place a competent attacker is going to stash his or her tools. If a toolkit is online, it is most likely encrypted or at least password protected to prevent dissemination, which would alert the community, resulting in the eventual lockdown of potential targets. This isn't to say that new, unpublished exploits are *not* online, but frankly it's often easier to build relationships with those in the know. Still, there's nothing wrong with having a nice hit list of public exploit sites, and Google is great at collecting those with simple queries that include the words *exploit, vulnerability,* or *vulnerable.* Google can also be used to locate source code by focusing on certain strings that appear in that type of code.

Locating potential targets with Google is a fairly straightforward process, requiring nothing more than a unique string presented by a vulnerable Web application. In some cases these strings can be culled from demonstration applications that a vendor provides. In other cases, an attacker might need to download the product or source code to locate a string to use in a Google query. Either way, a public Web application exploit announcement, combined with the power of Google, leaves little time for a defender to secure a vulnerable application or server.

CHAPTER 7

Ten Simple Security Searches That Work

INTRODUCTION

Although we see literally hundreds of Google searches throughout this book, sometimes it's nice to know there are a few searches that give good results just about every time. In the context of security work, we'll take a look at 10 searches that work fairly well during a security assessment, especially when combined with the *site* operator, which secures the first position in our list. As you become more and more comfortable with Google, you'll certainly add to this list, modifying a few searches and quite possibly deleting a few, but the searches here should serve as a very nice baseline for your own top 10 list. Without further ado, let's dig into some queries.

SITE

The *site* operator is absolutely invaluable during the information-gathering phase of an assessment. Combined with a host or domain name, this query presents results that can be overwhelming, to say the least. However, the *site* operator is meant to be used as a base search, not necessarily as a standalone search. Sure, it's possible (and not entirely discouraged) to scan through *every single* page of results from this query, but in most cases it's just downright impractical.

Important information can be gained from a straight-up site search, however. First, remember that Google lists the results in page-ranked order. In other words, the most popular pages float to the top. This means you can get a quick idea about what the rest of the Internet thinks is most worthwhile about a site. The implications of this information are varied, but at a basic level you can at least get an idea of the public image or consensus about an online presence by looking at what floats to the top. Outside the specific site search itself, it can be helpful to read into the context of links originating from other sites. If a link's text says something to the effect of "CompanyXYZ s***s!", there's a good chance that someone is discontent about CompanyXYZ.

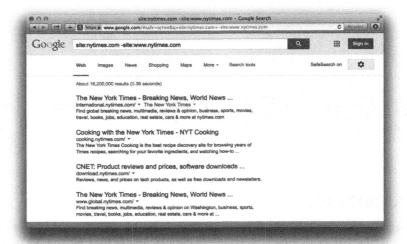

FIGURE 7.1

As we saw in Chapter 5, the site search can also be used to gather information about the servers and hosts that a target maintains. Using simple reduction techniques, we can quickly get an idea about a target's online presence. Consider the simple example of *site:nytimes.com –site: www.nytimes.com* shown in Figure 7.1.

This query effectively locates hosts on the nytimes.com domain other than www.nytimes.com. Just from a first pass, Figure 7.1 shows three hosts: theater. nytimes.com, www2.nytimes.com, salary.nytimes.com and realestate.nytimes. com. These may be hosts, or they may be subdomains. Further investigation would be required to determine this. Also remember to validate your Google results before unleashing your megascanner of choice.

INTITLE:INDEX.OF

intitle:index.of is the universal search for directory listings. Directory listings are chock-full of juicy details, as we saw in Chapter 3. Firing an *intitle:index.of* query against a target is fast and easy and could produce a killer payoff.

ERROR | WARNING

As we've seen throughout this book, error messages can reveal a great deal of information about a target. Often overlooked, error messages can provide insight into the application or operating system software a target is running, the architecture of the network the target is on, information about users on the system, and much more. Not only are error messages informative, they are

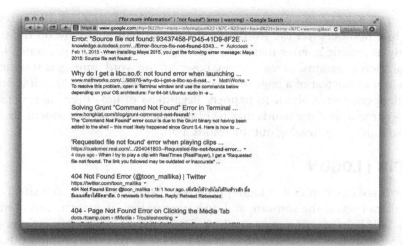

FIGURE 7.2

prolific. This query will take some playing with, and is best when combined with a *site* query. For example, a query of *("for more information" | "not found") (error | warning)* returns interesting results, as shown in Figure 7.2.

Unfortunately, some error messages don't actually display the word *error*, as shown in the SQL located with a query of *"access denied for user" "using password"* shown in Figure 7.3.

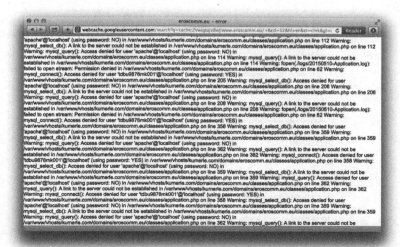

FIGURE 7.3

This error page reveals usernames, filenames, path information, IP addresses, and line numbers, yet the word *error* does not occur anywhere on the page. Nearly as prolific as error messages, warning messages can be generated from application programs. In some cases, however, the word *warning* is specifically written into the text of a page to alert the Web user that something important has happened or is about to happen. Regardless of how they are generated, pages containing these words may be of interest during an assessment, as long as you don't mind teasing out the results a bit.

LOGIN | LOGON

As we'll see in Chapter 8, a login portal is a "front door" to a Web site. Login portals can reveal the software and operating system of a target, and in many cases "self-help" documentation is linked from the main page of a login portal. These documents are designed to assist users who run into problems during the login process. Whether the user has forgotten a password or even a user-name, this documents can provide clues that might help an attacker, or in our case a security tester, gain access to the site.

Many times, documentation linked from login portals lists email addresses, phone numbers, or URLs of human assistants who can help a troubled user regain lost access. These assistants, or help desk operators, are perfect targets for a social engineering attack. Even the smallest security testing team should not be without a social engineering whiz that could talk an Eskimo out of his thermal underwear. The vast majority of all security systems have one common weakest link: a human behind a keyboard. The words *login* and *logon* are widely used on the Internet, occurring on millions of pages, as shown in Figure 7.4.

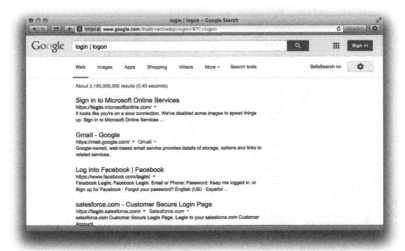

FIGURE 7.4

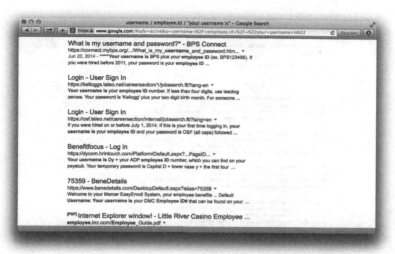

FIGURE 7.5

Also common is the phrase *login trouble* in the text of the page. A phrase like this is designed to steer wayward users who have forgotten their login credentials. This information is of course very valuable to attackers and pen testers alike.

USERNAME | USERID | EMPLOYEE.ID \ "YOUR USERNAME IS"

As we'll see in Chapter 9, there are many different ways to obtain a username from a target system. Even though a username is the less important half of most authentication mechanisms, it should at least be marginally protected from outsiders. Figure 7.5 shows that even sites that reveal very little information in the face of a barrage of probing Google queries, return many potentially interesting results to this query. To avoid implying anything negative about the target used in this example, some details of the Figure 7.5 have been edited.

The mere existence of the word *username* in a result is not indicative of a vulnerability, but results from this query provide a starting point for an attacker. Since there's no good reason to remove derivations of the word *username* from a site you protect, why not rely on this common set of words to at least get a foothold during an assessment?

PASSWORD | PASSCODE | "YOUR PASSWORD IS"

The word *password* is so common on the Internet, there are over a billion results for this one-word query. Launching a query for derivations of this word makes little sense unless you actually combine that search with the *site* operator.

FIGURE 7.6

During an assessment, it's very likely that results for this query combined with a *site* operator will include pages that provide help to users who have forgotten their passwords. In some cases, this query will locate pages that provide policy information about the *creation* of a password. This type of information can be used in an intelligent-guessing or even a brute-force campaign against a password field.

Despite how this query looks, it's quite uncommon for this type of query to return *actual* passwords. Passwords do exist on the Web, but this query isn't well suited for locating them. (We'll look at queries to locate passwords in Chapter 9.) Like the login portal and username queries, this query can provide an informational foothold into a system. Most often, this query should be used alongside a *site* operator, but with a little tweaking, the query can be used without *site* to illustrate the point, as shown in Figure 7.6. "Forgotten password" pages like these can be very informative.

ADMIN | ADMINISTRATOR

The word *administrator* is often used to describe the person in control of a network or system. There are so many references to the word on the Web that a query for *admin | administrator* weighs in at half a billion results. This suggests that these words have most likely been referred to on a site that you're assessing. However, the value of these and other words in a query does not lie in the number of results but in the contextual relevance of the words. Tweaking this query, with the addition of "change your" can return

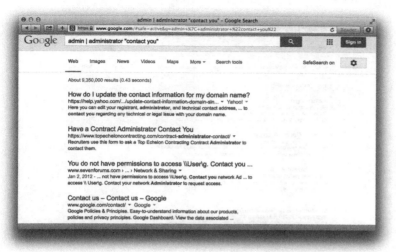

FIGURE 7.7

interesting results, even without the addition of a *site* operator, as shown in Figure 7.7.

The phrase *Contact your system administrator* is a fairly common phrase on the Web, as are several basic derivations. A query such as *"please contact your * administrator"* will return results that refer to local, company, site, department, server, system, network, database, email, and even tennis administrators. If a Web user is told to contact an administrator, odds are that there's data of at least moderate importance to a security tester.

The word *administrator* can also be used to locate administrative login pages, or login portals. (We'll take a closer look at login portal detection in Chapter 8.) A query for *"administrative login"* returns millions of results, many of which are administrative login pages. A security tester can profile Web servers using seemingly insignificant clues found on these types of login pages. Most login portals provide clues to an attacker about what software is in use on the server and act as a magnet, drawing attackers who are armed with an exploit for that particular type of software. As shown in Figure 7.8, many of the results for the combined admin query reveal administrative login pages.

Another interesting use of the *administrator* derivations is to search for them in the URL of a page using an *inurl* search. If the word *admin* is found in the hostname, a directory name, or a filename within a URL, there's a decent chance that the URL has some administrative function, making it interesting from a security standpoint.

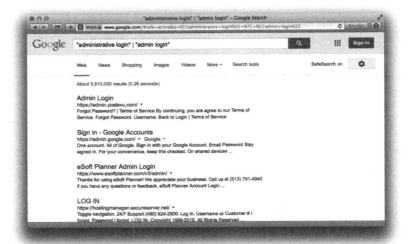

FIGURE 7.8

–EXT:HTML –EXT:HTM –EXT:SHTML –EXT:ASP –EXT:PHP

The *–ext:html –ext:htm –ext:shtml –ext:asp –ext:php* query uses *ext*, a synonym for the *filetype* operator, and is a negative query. It returns no results when used alone and should be combined with a *site* operator to work properly. The idea behind this query is to exclude some of the most common Internet file types in an attempt to find files that might be more interesting for our purposes.

As you'll see through this book, there are certainly lots of HTML, PHP, and ASP pages that reveal interesting information, but this chapter is about cutting to the chase, and that's what this query attempts to do. The documents returned by this search often have great potential for document grinding, which we'll explore in more detail in Chapter 10. The file extensions used in this search were selected very carefully. First, www.filext.com (one of the Internet's best resources for all known file extensions) was consulted to obtain a list of every known file extension. Each entry in the list of over 8000 file extensions was converted into a Google query using the *filetype* operator. For example, if we wanted to search for the PDF extension, we might use a query like *filetype:PDF* to get the number of known results on the Internet. This type of Google query was performed for each and every known file extension from filext.com, which can take quite some time, especially when done in accordance with Google Terms of Use agreement. Once the results were gathered, they were sorted in descending order by the number of hits.

A site search combined with a *negative* search for the top ten most common file types can lead you right to some potentially interesting documents. In some cases, this query will need to be refined, especially if the site uses a less

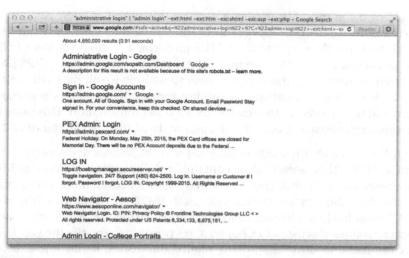

FIGURE 7.9

common server-generated file extension. For example, consider this query combined with a *site* operator, as shown in Figure 7.9. (To protect the identity of the target, certain portions of the Figure 7.9 have been edited.)

As revealed in the search results, this site uses the ASPX extension for some Web content. By adding *–ext:aspx* to the query and resubmitting it, that type of content is removed from the search results. This modified search reveals some interesting information, as shown in Figure 7.10.

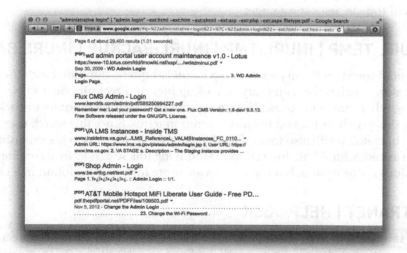

FIGURE 7.10

By adding a common file extension used on this site, after a few pages of mediocre results we discover a page full of interesting information. Result line 1 reveals that the site supports the HTTPS protocol, a secured version of HTTP used to protect sensitive information. The mere existence of the HTTPS protocol often indicates that this server houses something worth protecting. Result line 1 also reveals several nested subdirectories (/research/files/summaries) that could be explored or traversed to locate other information. This same line also reveals the existence of a PDF document dated the first quarter of 2003.

Result line 2 reveals the existence of what is most likely a development server named DEV. This server also contains subdirectories (/events/archives/strategiesNAM2003) that could be traversed to uncover more information. One of the subdirectory names, strategiesNAM2003, contains a "the string 2003," most likely a reference to the year 2003. Using the incremental substitution technique discussed in Chapter 3, it's possible to modify the year in this directory name to uncover similarly named directories. Result line 2 also reveals the existence of an attendee list that could be used to discover usernames, email addresses, and so on.

Result line 3 reveals another machine name, JOBS, which contains a ColdFusion application that accepts parameters. Depending on the nature and security of this application, an attack based on user input might be possible. Result line 4 reveals new directory names, /help/emp, which could be traversed or fed into other third-party assessment applications.

The results continue, but the point is that once common, purposefully placed files are removed from a search, interesting information tends to float to the top. This type of reduction can save an attacker or a security technician a good deal of time in assessing a target.

INURL:TEMP | INURL:TMP | INURL:BACKUP | INURL.BAK

The *inurl:temp | inurl:tmp | inurl:backup | inurl:bak* query, combined with the *site* operator, searches for temporary or backup files or directories on a server. Although there are many possible-naming conventions for temporary or backup files, this search focuses on the most common terms. Since this search uses the *inurl* operator, it will also locate files that contain these terms as file extensions, such as index.html.bak, for example. Modifying this search to focus on file extensions is one option, but these terms are more interesting if found in a URL.

INTRANET | HELP.DESK

The term *intranet*, despite more specific technical meanings, has become a generic term that describes a network confined to a small group. In most cases the term *intranet* describes a closed or private network, unavailable to the general public. However, many sites have configured portals that allow access to an intranet from the Internet, bringing this typically closed network one step closer to potential attackers.

In rare cases, private intranets have been discovered on the public Internet due to a network device misconfiguration. In these cases, network administrators were completely unaware that their private networks were accessible to anyone via the Internet. Most often, an Internet-connected intranet is only partially accessible from the outside. In these cases, filters are employed that only allow access to certain pages from specific addresses, presumably inside a facility or campus. There are two major problems with this type of configuration. First, it's an administrative nightmare to keep track of the access rights of specific pages. Second, this is not true access control. This type of restriction can be bypassed very easily if an attacker gains access to a local proxy server, bounces a request off a local misconfigured Web server, or simply compromises a machine on the same network as trusted intranet users. Unfortunately, it's nearly impossible to provide a responsible example of this technique in action. Each example we considered for this section was too easy for an attacker to reconstruct with a few simple Google queries.

Help desks have a bad reputation of being, well, too helpful. Since the inception of help desks, hackers have been donning alternate personalities in an attempt to gain sensitive information from unsuspecting technicians. Recently, help desk procedures have started to address the hacker threat by insisting that technicians validate callers before attempting to assist them. Most help desk workers will (or should) ask for identifying information such as usernames, Social Security numbers, employee numbers, and even PIN numbers to properly validate callers' identities. Some procedures are better than others, but for the most part, today's help desk technicians are at least *aware* of the potential threat that is posed by an imposter.

In Chapter 4, we discussed ways Google can be used to harvest the identification information a help desk may require, but the *intranet | help.desk* query is not designed to bypass help desk procedures but rather to locate pages describing help desk procedures. When this query is combined with a *site* search, the results could indicate the location of a help desk (Web page, telephone number, or the like), the information that might be requested by help desk technicians (which an attacker could gather before calling), and in many cases links that describe troubleshooting procedures. Self-help documentation is often rather verbose, and a crafty attacker can use the information in these documents to profile a target network or server. There are exceptions to every rule, but odds are that this query, combined with the *site* operator, will dig up information about a target that can feed a future attack.

SUMMARY

This list may not be perfect, but these 10 searches should serve you well as you seek to compile your own list of killer searches. It's important to realize that a search that works against one target might not work well against other targets. Keep track of the searches that work for you, and try to reach some common ground about what works and what doesn't. Automated tools, discussed in Chapters 11 and 12, can be used to feed longer lists of Google queries such as those found in the Google Hacking Database, but in some cases, simpler might be better. If you're having trouble finding common ground in some queries that work for you, don't hesitate to keep them in a list for use in one of the automated tools that we'll discuss later.

CHAPTER 8

Tracking Down Web Servers, Login Portals, and Network Hardware

INTRODUCTION

Penetration (pen) testers are sometimes thought of as professional hackers since they essentially break into their customers' networks in an attempt to locate, document, and ultimately help resolve security flaws in a system or network. However, pen testers and hackers differ quite a bit in several ways.

For example, most penetration testers are provided with specific instructions about which networks and systems they will be testing. Their targets are specified for many reasons, but in all cases, their targets are clearly defined or bounded in some fashion. Hackers, on the other hand, have the luxury of selecting from a wider target base. Depending on his or her motivations and skill level, the attacker might opt to select a target based on known exploits at his or her disposal. This reverses the model used by pen testers, and as such it affects the structure we will use to explore the topic of Google hacking. The techniques we'll explore in the next few chapters are most often employed by hackers – the "bad guys."

Penetration testers have access to the techniques we'll explore in these chapters, but in many cases these techniques are too cumbersome for use during a vulnerability assessment, when time is of the essence. Security professionals often use specialized tools that perform these tasks in a much more streamlined fashion, but these tools make lots of noise and often overlook the simplest form of information leakage that Google is so capable of revealing – and revealing in a way that's nearly impossible to catch on the "radar." The techniques we'll examine here are used on a daily basis to locate and explore the systems and networks attached to the Internet, so it's important that we explore how these techniques are used to better understand the level of exposure and how that exposure can be properly mitigated.

The techniques we explore in this chapter are used to locate and analyze the front-end systems on an Internet-connected network. We look at ways an attacker can profile Web servers using seemingly insignificant clues found with Google queries. Next, we'll look at methods used to locate login portals, the literal front door of most Web sites. As we will see, some login portals provide administrators of a system an access point for performing various administrative functions. Most login portals provide clues to an attacker about what software is in use on the server, and draws the attention of attackers that are armed with an exploit for that particular type of software. We round out the chapter by showing techniques that can be used to locate all sorts of network devices – firewalls, routers, network printers, and even Web cameras.

LOCATING AND PROFILING WEB SERVERS

If an attacker hasn't already decided on a target, he might begin with a Google search for specific targets that match an exploit at his disposal. He might focus specifically on the operating system, the version and brand of Web server software, default configurations, vulnerable scripts, or any combination of factors.

There are many different ways to locate a server. The most common way is with a simple portscan. Using a tool such as Nmap, a simple scan of port 80 across a class C network will expose potential Web servers. Integrated tools such as Nessus, OpenVAS, Qualys, or Retina will run some type of portscan, followed by a series of security tests. These functions can be replicated with Google queries, although in most cases the results are nowhere near as effective as the results from a well-thoughtout vulnerability scanner or Web assessment tool. Remember, though, that Google queries are less obvious and provide a degree of separation between an attacker and a target. Also remember that hackers can use Google hacking techniques to find systems you may be charged with protecting. The bottom line is that it's important to understand the capabilities of the Google hacker and realize the role Google can play in an attacker's methodology.

Directory Listings

We discussed directory listings in Chapter 3, but the importance of directory listings with regard to profiling methods is important. The *server* tag at the bottom of a directory listing can provide explicit detail about the type of Web server software that's running. If an attacker has an exploit for Apache 2.4.12 running on a UNIX server, a query such as *server.at "Apache/2.4.12"* will locate servers that host a directory listing with an Apache 2.4.12 *server* tag.

Not all Web servers place this tag at the bottom of directory listings, but most Apache derivatives turn on this feature by default. Other platforms, such as Microsoft's Internet Information Server (IIS), display server tags as well, as a query for *"Microsoft-IIS/7.0 server at"*.

When searching for these directory tags, keep in mind that your syntax is very important. There are many irrelevant results from a query for *"Microsoft-IIS/7.0""server at"*, whereas a query like *"Microsoft-IIS/7.0 server at"* provides very relevant results. Since we've already covered directory listings, we won't dwell on it here. Refer to Chapter 3 if you need for directory listings.

Web Server Software Error Messages

Error messages contain a lot of useful information, but in the context of locating specific servers, we can use portions of various error messages to locate servers running specific software versions. We'll begin our discussion by looking at error messages that are generated by the Web server software itself.

Microsoft IIS

The best way to find error messages is to figure out what messages the server is capable of generating. You could gather these messages by examining the server source code or configuration files or by actually generating the errors on the server yourself. The best way to get this information from IIS is by examining the source code of the error pages themselves.

IIS 5.0 and 6.0, by default, display static Hypertext Transfer Protocol (HTTP)/1.1 error messages when the server encounters some sort of problem. These error pages are stored by default in the *%SYSTEMROOT%\help\iisHelp\common* directory. These files are essentially Hypertext Markup language (HTML) files named by the type of error they produce, such as 400.htm, 401-1.htm, 501. htm, and so on. By analyzing these files, we can come up with trends and commonalities between the pages that are essential for effective Google searching. For example, the file that produces 400 error pages, 400.htm, contains a line (line 12) that looks like this:

```
<title>The page cannot be found</title>
```

This is a dead giveaway for an effective *intitle* query such as *intitle:""The page cannot be found"*. Unfortunately, this search yields (as you might guess) far too many results. We'll need to dig deeper into the 400.htm file to get more clues about what to look for. Lines 65–88 of 400.htm are shown here:

65.   <p>Please try the following:</p>

66.   <ul>

67.   <li>If you typed the page address in the Address bar, make sure that it is

spelled correctly.</li>

68.

69.   <li>Open the

70.

71.   <script language="JavaScript">

72. <!--

73.   if (!((window.navigator.userAgent.indexOf("MSIE") > 0) &&

(window.navigator.appVersion.charAt(0) == "2")))

74.   {

75.   Homepage();

76.   }

77.   -->

78.   </script>

79.

80.   home page, and then look for links to the information you want.</li>

81.

82.   <li>Click the

83.   <a href="javascript:history.back(1)">

84. Back</a> button to try another link.</li>

85. </ul>

86.

87. <h2 style="COLOR:000000; FONT: 8pt/11pt verdana">HTTP
400 - Bad Request

88. Internet Information Services</h2>

The phrase *"Please try the following"* in line 65 exists in *every single* error file in this directory, making it a perfect candidate for part of a good base search. This line could effectively be reduced to *"please * * following."* Line 88 shows another phrase that appears in every error document; *"Internet Information Services,"* These are "golden terms" to use to search for IIS HTTP/1.1 error pages that Google has crawled. A query such as *intitle:"The page cannot be found" "please * * following" "Internet * Services"* can be used to search for IIS servers that present a 400 error page.

Looking at this cached page carefully, you'll notice that the actual error code itself is printed on the page, about halfway down. This error line is also printed on each of IIS's error pages, making for another good limiter for our searching. The line on the page begins with *"HTTP Error 404,"* which might seem out of place, considering we were searching for a 400 error code, not a 404 error code, as seen in Figures 8.1 and 8.2. This occurs because several IIS error pages produce similar pages. Although commonalities are often good for Google searching, they could lead to some confusion and produce ineffective results if we are searching for a specific, less benign error page. It's obvious that we'll need to sort out exactly what's what in these error page files.

These page titles, used in an *intitle* search, combined with the other golden IIS error searches, make for very effective searches, locating all sorts of IIS servers that generate all sorts of telling error pages. To troll for IIS servers with the esoteric 404.1 error page, try a query such *as intitle:"The Web site cannot be found" "please * * following"*. A more common error can be found with a query such as *intitle:"The page cannot be displayed" "Internet Information Services" "please * * following"*, which is very effective because this error page is shown for many different error codes.

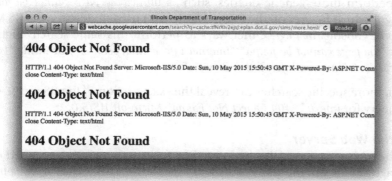

FIGURE 8.1

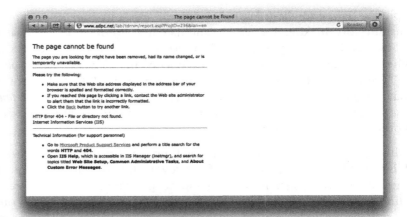

FIGURE 8.2

In addition to displaying the default static HTTP/1.1 error pages, IIS can be configured to display custom error messages, configured via the Management Console. An example of this type of custom error page. This type of functionality makes the job of the Google hacker a bit more difficult since there is no apparent way to home in on a customized error page. However, some error messages, including 400, 403.9, 411, 414, 500, 500.11, 500.14, 500.15, 501, 503, and 505 pages, cannot be customized. In terms of Google hacking, this means that there is no easy way an IIS 6.0 server can prevent displaying the static HTTP/1.1 error pages we so effectively found previously. This opens the door for locating these servers through Google, even if the server has been configured to display custom error pages.

Besides trolling through the IIS error pages looking for exact phrases, we can also perform more generic queries, such as *intitle:"the page cannot be found" inetmgr"*, which focuses on the fairly unique term used to describe the IIS Management console, *inetmgr*. Other ways to perform this same search might be *intitle:"the page cannot be found" "internet information services"*, or *intitle:"Under construction" "Internet Information Services"*.

Other, more specific searches can reveal the exact version of the IIS server, such as a query for *intext:" "404 Object Not Found" Microsoft-IIS/5.0*.

Apache Web Server
Apache Web servers can also be located by focusing on server-generated error messages. Some generic searches such as *"Apache/2.4.12 Server at""-intitle:index. of intitle:inf"* or *"Apache/2.4.12 Server at" -intitle:index.of intitle:error* can be used to locate servers that might be advertising their server version via an info or error message.

A query such as *"Apache/2.4.12" intitle:"Object not found!"* will locate Apache 2.4.12 Web servers that presented this error message. Although there might be nothing wrong with throwing queries around looking for commonalities and good base searches, we've already seen in the IIS section that it's more effective to consult the server software itself for search clues. Most Apache installations rely on a configuration file called *httpd.conf*. Searching through Apache 2.0.40's *httpd.conf* file reveals the location of the HTML templates for error messages. The referenced files (which follow) are located in the Web root directory, such as */error/http_BAD_REQUEST.html.var*, which refers to the */var/www/error* directory on the file system:

```
ErrorDocument 400 /error/HTTP_BAD_REQUEST.html.var

ErrorDocument 401 /error/HTTP_UNAUTHORIZED.html.var

ErrorDocument 403 /error/HTTP_FORBIDDEN.html.var

ErrorDocument 404 /error/HTTP_NOT_FOUND.html.var

ErrorDocument 405 /error/HTTP_METHOD_NOT_ALLOWED.html.var

ErrorDocument 408 /error/HTTP_REQUEST_TIME_OUT.html.var

ErrorDocument 410 /error/HTTP_GONE.html.var

ErrorDocument 411 /error/HTTP_LENGTH_REQUIRED.html.var

ErrorDocument 412 /error/HTTP_PRECONDITION_FAILED.html.var

ErrorDocument 413 /error/HTTP_REQUEST_ENTITY_TOO_LARGE.html.var

ErrorDocument 414 /error/HTTP_REQUEST_URI_TOO_LARGE.html.var

ErrorDocument 415 /error/HTTP_SERVICE_UNAVAILABLE.html.var

ErrorDocument 500 /error/HTTP_INTERNAL_SERVER_ERROR.html.var

ErrorDocument 501 /error/HTTP_NOT_IMPLEMENTED.html.var

ErrorDocument 502 /error/HTTP_BAD_GATEWAY.html.var

ErrorDocument 503 /error/HTTP_SERVICE_UNAVAILABLE.html.var

ErrorDocument 506 /error/HTTP_VARIANT_ALSO_VARIES.html.var
```

Taking a look at one of these template files, we can see recognizable HTML code and variable listings that show the construction of an error page. The file itself is divided into sections by language. The English portion of the *HTTP_NOT_FOUND.html.var* file is shown here:

Content-language: en Content-type: text/html Body:----------en-- < !—#set var = "TITLE" value = "Object not found!" —> <!—#include virtual = "include/ top.html" —>

The requested URL was not found on this server.

```
<!--#if expr="$HTTP_REFERER" -->

The link on the <a href="<!--#echo encoding="url" var="HTTP_REFERER"--

>">referring

  page</a> seems to be wrong or outdated. Please inform the author of

  <a href="<!--#echo encoding="url" var="HTTP_REFERER"-->">that page</a>

  about the error.

<!--#else -->

  If you entered the URL manually please check your

  spelling and try again.

<!--#endif -->
```

<!—#include virtual="include/bottom.html" —>

Notice that the sections of the error page are clearly labeled, making it easy to translate into Google queries. The *TITLE* variable, shown near the top of the listing, indicates that the text *"Object not found!"* will be displayed in the browser's title bar. When this file is processed and displayed in a Web browser. However, Google hacking is not always this easy. A search for *intitle:"Object not found!"* is too generic.

These results are not what we're looking for. To narrow our results, we need a better base search. Constructing our base search from the template files included with the Apache 2.0 source code not only enables us to locate all the potential error messages the server is capable of producing, it also shows us how those messages are translated into other languages, resulting in very solid multilingual base searches.

The *HTTP_NOT_FOUND.html.var* file listed previously referred to two *virtual include* lines, one near the top (*include/top.html*) and one near the bottom (*include/bottom.html*). These lines instruct Apache to read and insert the contents of these two files (located in our case in the */var/www/error/ include* directory) into the current file. The following code lists the contents of the *bottom.html* file and shows some subtleties that will help construct that perfect base search:

```
</dd></dl><dl><dd><!--#include virtual="../contact.html.var" --

></dd></dl><h2>Error <!--#echo encoding="none" var="REDIRECT_STATUS" --

></h2> <dl><dd><address><a href="/"><!--#echo encoding="url"

var="SERVER_NAME" --></a> <br /><!--#config timefmt="%c" --><small><!--

#echo encoding="none" var="DATE_LOCAL" --></small><br /><small><!--#echo

encoding="none" var="SERVER_SOFTWARE" --></small>

</address></dd></dl></body></html>
```

First, notice line 4, which will display the word "*Error*" on the page. Although this might seem very generic, it's an important subtlety that would keep results from displaying. Line 2 shows that another file (/var/www/error/contact.html. var) is read and included into this file. The contents of this file, listed as follows, contain more details that we can include into our base search:

1. Content-language: en
2. Content-type: text/html
3. Body:----------en--
4. **If you think this is a server error, please contact the** <a href = "mailto: < !--#echo encoding = "none" var = "SERVER_ADMIN" -- >" > **webmaster** < /a>
5. ----------en--

This file, like the file that started this whole "include chain," is broken up into sections by language. The portion of this file listed here shows yet another unique string we can use. We'll select a fairly unique piece of this line, "*think this is a server error*," as a portion of our base search instead of just the word *error*, which we used initially to remove some false positives. The other part of our base search, *intitle:"Object not found!"*, was originally found in the /error/ http_BAD_REQUEST.html.var file. The final base search for this file then becomes *intitle:"Object Not Found!" "think this is a server error"*, which returns more accurate results.

Now that we've found a good base search for one error page, we can automate the query-hunting process to determine good base searches for the other error pages referenced in the *httpd.conf* file, helping us create solid base searches for each and every default Apache (2.0) error page. The *contact.html.var* file that we saw previously is included in each and every Apache 2.0 error page via the *bottom.html* file. This means that "*think this is a server error*" will work for all the different error pages that Apache 2.0 will produce. The other critical element to our search was the *intitle* search, which we could *grep* for in each of the error files.

While we're at it, we should also try to grab a snippet of the text that is printed in each of the error pages, remembering that in some cases a more specific search might be needed. Using some basic shell commands, we can isolate both the title of an error page and the text that might appear on the error page:

```
grep -h -r "Content-language: en" * -A 10 | grep -A5 "TITLE" | grep -v virtual
```

Instead of searching for English messages only, we could search for errors in other Apache-supported languages by simply replacing the *Content-language* string in the previous *grep* command from *en* to either *de*, *es*, *fr*, or *sv*, for German, Spanish, French, or Swedish, respectively.

To use this table, simply supply the text in the Error Page Title column as an *intitle* search and a portion of the text column as an additional phrase in the search query. Since some of the text is lengthy, you might need to select a unique portion of the text or replace common words with an asterisk, which will reduce your search query to the 10-word limit imposed on Google queries. For example, a good query for the first line of the table might be *"response from * upstream server." intitle:"Bad Gateway!"*. Alternately, you could also rely on the *"think this is a server error"* phrase combined with a title search, such as *"think this is a server error" intitle:"Bad Gateway!"*. Different versions of Apache will display slightly different error messages, but the process of locating and creating solid base searches from software source code is something you should get comfortable with to stay ahead of the ever-changing software market.

This technique can be expanded to find Apache servers in other languages by reviewing the rest of the *contact.html.var* file. Because these sentences and phrases are included in every Apache error message, they should appear *in the text* of *every error page* that the Apache server produces, making them ideal for base searches. It is possible (and fairly easy) to modify these error pages to provide a more polished appearance when a user encounters an error; but remember, hackers have different motivations. Some are simply interested in locating particular versions of a server, perhaps to exploit. Using these criteria, there is no shortage of servers on the Internet that are using these default error phrases, and by extension may have a default, less-secured configuration.

Besides Apache and IIS, other servers (and other versions of these servers) can be located by searching for server-produced error messages, but we're trying to keep this book just a bit thinner than your local yellow pages, so we'll draw the line at just these two servers.

Application Software Error Messages

The error messages we've looked at so far have all been generated by the Web server itself. In many cases, applications running on the Web server can generate errors that reveal information about the server as well. There are untold thousands of Web applications on the Internet, each of which can generate any number of error messages. Dedicated Web assessment tools such as SPI Dynamic's WebInspect excel at performing detailed Web application assessments, making it seem a bit pointless to troll Google for application error messages. However, we search for error message output throughout this book simply because the data contained in error messages should not be overlooked.

We've looked at various error messages in previous chapters, and we'll see more error messages in later chapters, but let's take a quick look at how error messages can help profile a Web server and its applications. Admittedly, we will hardly scratch the surface of this topic, but we'll make an effort to stimulate your thinking about Google's ability to locate these sometimes very telling error messages.

One query, *"Fatal error: Call to undefined function" -reply -the –next*, will locate Active Server Page (ASP) error messages. These messages often reveal information about the database software in use on the server as well as information about the application that caused the error.

Although this ASP message is fairly benign, some ASP error messages are much more revealing. Consider the query *"ASP.NET_SessionId" "data source = "*, which locates unique strings found in ASP.NET application state dumps. These dumps reveal all sorts of information about the running application and the Web server that hosts that application. An advanced attacker could use encrypted password data and variable information in these stack traces to subvert the security of the application and perhaps the Web server itself.

Hypertext Preprocessor (PHP) application errors are fairly commonplace. They can reveal all sorts of information that an attacker can use to profile a server. One very common error can be found with a query such as *intext:"Warning: Failed opening" include_path*.

CGI programs often reveal information about the Web server and its applications in the form of environment variable dumps.

This screen shows information about the Web server and the client that connected to the page when the data was produced. Since Google's bot crawls pages for us, one way to find these CGI environment pages is to focus on the trail left by the bot, reflected in these pages as the *"HTTP_FROM = googlebot"* line. We can search for pages like this with a query such as *"HTTP_FROM = googlebot" googlebot.com "Server_Software"*. These pages are dynamically generated, which means that you must look at Google's cache to see the document as it was crawled.

To locate good base searches for a particular application, it's best to look at the source code of that application. Using the techniques we've explored so far, it's simple to create these searches.

Default Pages

Another way to locate specific types of servers or Web software is to search for default Web pages. Most Web software, including the Web server software itself, ships with one or more default or test pages. These pages can make it easy for a site administrator to test the installation of a Web server or application. By providing a simple page to test, the administrator can simply connect to his own Web server with a browser to validate that the Web software was installed correctly. Some operating systems even come with Web server software already installed. In this case, the owner of the machine might not even realize that a Web server is running on his machine. This type of casual behavior on the part of the owner will lead an attacker to rightly assume that the Web software is not well maintained and is, by extension, insecure. By further extension, the attacker can also assume that the entire operating system of the server might be vulnerable by virtue of poor maintenance.

In some cases, Google crawls a Web server while it is in its earliest stages of installation, still displaying a set of default pages. In these cases there's generally a short window of time between the moment when Google crawls the site and when the intended content is actually placed on the server. This means that there could be a disparity between what the live page is displaying and what Google's cache displays. This makes little difference from a Google hacker's perspective, since even the past existence of a default page is enough for profiling purposes. Remember, we're essentially searching Google's cached version of a page when we submit a query. Regardless of the reason a server has default pages installed, there's an attacker somewhere who will eventually show interest in a machine displaying default pages found with a Google search.

Notice that the administrator's email is generic as well, indicating that not a lot of attention was paid to detail during the installation of this server. These default pages do not list the version number of the server, which is a required piece of information for a successful attack. It is possible, however, that an attacker could search for specific variations in these default pages to find specific ranges of server versions.

Using these subtle differences to our advantage, we can use specific Google queries to locate servers with these default pages, indicating that they are most likely running a specific version of Apache.

Although each version of IIS displays distinct default Web pages, in some cases service packs or hotfixes could alter the content of a default page. In these cases, the subtle page changes can be incorporated into the search to find not only the operating system version and Web server version, but also the service pack level and security patch level. This information is invaluable to an attacker bent on hacking not only the Web server, but hacking beyond the Web server and into the operating system itself. In most cases, an attacker with control on the operating system can wreak more havoc on a machine than a hacker who controls only the Web server.

Default Documentation

Web server software often ships with manuals and documentation that end up in the Web directories. An attacker could use this documentation to either profile or locate Web software.

In most cases, default documentation does not as accurately portray the server version as well as error messages or default pages, but this information can certainly be used to locate targets and to gain an understanding of the potential security posture of the server. If the server administrator has forgotten to delete the default documentation, an attacker has every reason to believe that other details such as security have been overlooked as well.

In most cases, specialized programs such as CGI scanners or Web application assessment tools are better suited for finding these default pages and programs, but if Google has crawled the pages (for example, from a link on a default main page), you'll be able to locate these pages with Google queries.

LOCATING LOGIN PORTALS

Login portal is a term I use to describe a Web page that serves as a "front door" to a Web site. Login portals are designed to allow access to specific features or functions after a user logs in. Google hackers search for login portals as a way to profile the software that's in use on a target, and to locate links and documentation that might provide useful information for an attack. In addition, if an attacker has an exploit for a particular piece of software, and that software provides a login portal, the attacker can use Google queries to locate potential targets.

Some login portals, like the one shown in Figure 8.3, captured with *"microsoft outlook" "web access" version*, are obviously default pages provided by the software manufacturer – in this case, Microsoft. Just as an attacker can get an idea of the potential security of a target by simply looking for default pages, a default login portal can indicate that the technical skill of the server's administrators is generally low, revealing that the security of the site will most likely be

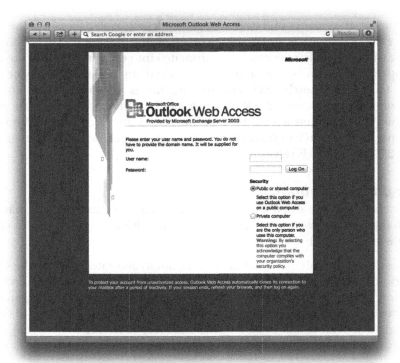

FIGURE 8.3

poor as well. To make matters worse, default login portals like the one shown in Figure 8.4, indicate the software revision of the program. An attacker can use this information to search for known vulnerabilities in that software version.

By following links from the login portal, an attacker can often gain access to other information about the target. The Outlook Web Access portal is particularly renowned for this type of information leak, because it provides an anonymous public access area that can be viewed without logging in to the mail system. This public access area sometimes provides access to a public directory or to broadcast emails that can be used to gather usernames or information, as shown in Figure 8.2.

Some login portals provide more details than others. As shown in Figure 8.4, provides a great deal of information about the server, including server software version and revision, application software version and revision, software upgrade date, and server uptime. This type of information is very handy for an attacker staging an attack against the server.

Login portals provide great information for use during a vulnerability assessment. Chapter 4 provides more details on getting the most from these pages.

FIGURE 8.4

USING AND LOCATING VARIOUS WEB UTILITIES

Google is amazing and very flexible, but it certainly can't do *everything*. Some things are much easier when you don't use Google. Tasks like WHOIS lookups, "pings," traceroutes, and portscans are much easier when performed *outside* of Google. There is a wealth of tools available that can perform these functions, but with a bit of creative Googling, it's possible to perform all of these arduous functions and more, preserving the level of anonymity Google hackers have come to expect. Consider a tool called the Network Query Tool (NQT), shown in Figure 8.5.

Default installations of NQT allow any Web user to perform Internet Protocol (IP) hostname and address lookups, Domain Name Server (DNS) queries, WHOIS queries, port testing, and traceroutes. This is a Web-based application, meaning that any user who can view the page can generally perform these functions against just about any target. This is a very handy tool for any security person, and for good reason. NQT functions appear to originate from the site hosting the NQT application. The Web server masks the real address of the user. The use of an anonymous proxy server would further mask the user's identity.

We can use Google to locate servers hosting the NQT program with a very simple query. The NQT program is usually called nqt.php, and in its default configuration displays the title "Network Query Tool." A simple query like *inurl:nqt.php intitle:"Network Query Tool"* returns many results, as shown in Figure 8.6.

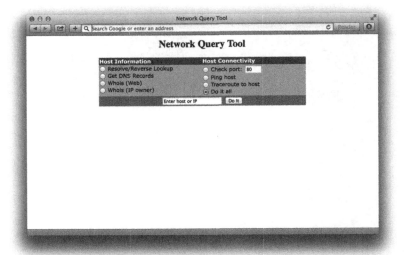

FIGURE 8.5

After submitting this query, it's a simple task to simply click on the results pages to locate a working NQT program. However, the NQT program accepts remote POSTS, which means it's possible to send an NQT "command" from your Web server to the *foo.com* server, which would execute the NQT "command" on your behalf. If this seems pointless, consider the fact that this would

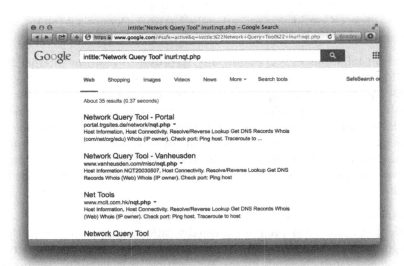

FIGURE 8.6

allow for simple extension of NQT's layout and capabilities. We could, for example, easily craft an NQT "rotator" that would execute NQT commands against a target, first bouncing it off an Internet NQT server. Let's take a look at how that might work.

First, we'll scrape the results page shown in Figure 8.5, creating a list of sites that host NQT. Consider the following Linux/Mac OS X command:

```
lynx -dump "

http://www.google.com/search?q=inurl:nqt.php+%22Network+\

Query+Tool%22&num=100" | grep "nqt.php$" | grep -v google |

awk '{print $2}' | sort –u
```

This command grabs 100 results of the Google query *inurl:nqt.php intitle:"Network Query Tool"*, locates the word *nqt.php* at the end of a line, removes any line that contains the word *google*, prints the second field in the list (which is the URL of the NQT site), and uniquely sorts that list. This command will not catch NQT URLs that contain parameters (since *nqt.php* will not be the last word in the link), but it produces clean output that might look something like this:

```
http://bevmo.dynsample.org/uptime/nqt.php

http://biohazard.sifsample7.com/nqt.php

http://cahasample.com/nqt.php

http://samplehost.net/resources/nqt.php

http://linux.sample.nu/phpwebsite_v1/nqt.php

http://noc.bogor.indo.samplenet.id/nqt.php

http://noc.cbn.samplenet.id/nqt.php

http://noc.neksample.org/nqt.php

http://portal.trgsample.de/network/nqt.php
```

We could dump this output into a file by appending >> *nqtfile.txt* to the end of the previous *sort* command. Now that we have a working list of NQT servers, we'll need a copy of the NQT code that produces the interface. This interface, with its buttons and *"enter host or IP"* field, will serve as the interface for our "rotator" program. Getting a copy of this interface is as easy as viewing the source of an existing *nqt.php* Web page (say, from the list of sites in the *nqtfile. txt* file), and saving the HTML content to a file we'll call *rotator.php* on our own Web server. At this point, we have two files in the same directory of our Web server – an *nqtfile.txt* file containing a list of NQT servers, and a *rotator.php* file that contains the HTML source of NQT. We'll be replacing a single line in the *rotator.php* file to create our "rotator" program. This line, which is the beginning of the NQT input form, reads:

```
<form method="post" action="/nqt.php">
```

This line indicates that once the "Do it" button is pressed, data will be sent to a script called nqt.php. If we were to modify this form field to <form method = "post" action = "http://foo.com/nqt.php">, our rotator program would send the NQT command to the NQT program located at foo.com, which would execute it on our behalf. We're going to take this one step further, inserting PHP code that will read a random site from the nqtfile.txt program, inserting it into the form line for us. This code might look something like this (lines numbered for clarity):

```
82. <?php

83.2.    $array = file("./nqtsites.txt");

84.

85.3.    $site=substr($array[rand(0,count($array)-1)],0,-1);

86.

87.4.    print "<form method=\"post\" action=$site><br>";

88.

89.5.    print "Using NQT Site: $site for this session.<br>";

90.

91.6.    print "Reload this page for a new NQT site.<br><br>";

92.

93. ?> This PHP code segment is meant to replace the <form method="post"
```

    action="/nqt.php">

lines in the original NQT HTML code. Line 1 indicates that a PHP code segment is about to begin. Since the rest of the *rotator.php* file is HTML, this line, as well as line 7 that terminates the PHP code segment, is required. Line 2 reads our *nqtsites.txt* file, assigning each line in the file (a URL to an NQT site) to an array element. Line 3, included as a separate line for readability, assigns one random line from the *nqtsites.txt* program to the variable *$site*. Line 4 outputs the modified version of the original *form* line, modifying the action target to point to a random remote NQT site. Lines 5 and 6 simply output informative messages about the NQT site that was selected, and instructions for loading a new NQT site. The next line in the *rotator.php* script would be the *table* line that draws the main NQT table.

Our rotator program looks very similar to the standard NQT program interface, with the addition of the two initial lines of text. However, when the "check port" box is checked, www.microsoft.com is entered into the host field, and the Do It button is clicked, we are whisked away to the results page on a remote NQT server that displays the results – port 80 is, in fact, open and accepting connections, as shown in Figure 8.7.

This example is designed to suggest that Google can be used to supplement the use of many Web-based applications. All that's required is a bit of Google know-how and a healthy dose of creativity.

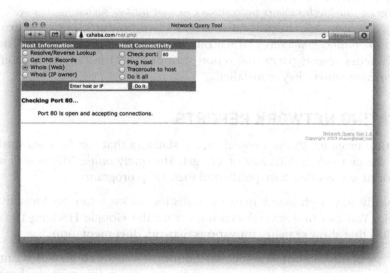

FIGURE 8.7

TARGETING WEB-ENABLED NETWORK DEVICES

Google can also be used to detect the presence of many Web-enabled network devices. Many network devices come preinstalled with a Web interface to allow an administrator to query the status of the device or to change device settings with a Web browser. While this is convenient, and can even be primitively secured through the use of a Secure Sockets Layer (SSL)-enabled connection, if the Web interface of a device is crawled with Google, even the mere existence of that device can add to a silently created network map. For example, a query like *intitle:"BorderManager information alert"* can reveal the existence of a Novell BorderManager Proxy/Firewall server.

A crafty attacker could use the mere existence of this device to craft his attack against the target network. For example, if this device is acting as a proxy server, the attacker might attempt to use it to gain access to machines inside a trusted network by bouncing connections off this server. Additionally, an attacker might search for any public vulnerabilities for this product in an attempt to exploit this device directly. Although many different devices can be located in this way, it's generally easier to harvest IP and network data using the output from network statistical programs as we'll see in the next section. To get an idea of the types of devices that can be located with this technique, consider queries like *"Version Info" "BootVersion" "Internet Settings"*, which locate Belkin Cable/DSL routers; *intitle:"wbem" compaq login*, which locates HP Insight Management Agents; *intitle:"lantronix web-manager"*, which locates Lantronix Web managers; *inurl:tech-support inurl:show Cisco* or *intitle:"switch home page" "cisco systems" "Telnet - to"*, which locates various Cisco products; or *intitle:"axis storpoint CD" intitle:"ip address"*, which can locate Axis StorPoint servers. Each of these queries reveals pages that report various bits of information about the networks on which they're installed.

LOCATING NETWORK REPORTS

The ntop program shows network traffic statistics that can be used to determine the network architecture of a target. The query *intitle:"Welcome to ntop!"* will locate servers that have publicized their ntop programs.

Practically any Web-based network statistics package can be located with Google. You can find several examples from the Google Hacking Database (GHDB) that show searches for various network documentation.

This type of information is a huge asset during a security audit, which can save a lot of time, but realize that any information found in this manner should be validated before using it in any type of finished report.

LOCATING NETWORK HARDWARE

It's not uncommon for a network-connected device to have a Web page of some sort. If that device is connected to the Internet and a link to that device's Web page ever existed, there's a good chance that that page is in Google's database, waiting to be located with a crafty query. As we discussed in Chapter 5, these pages can reveal information about the target network. This type of information can play a very important role in mapping a target network.

All types of devices can be connected to a network. These devices, ranging from switches and routers to printers and even firewalls, are considered great finds for any attacker interested in network reconnaissance, but some devices such as Webcams are interesting finds for an attacker as well.

In most cases, a network-connected Webcam is not considered a security threat but more a source of entertainment for any Web surfer. Keep a few things in mind, however. First, some companies consider it trendy and cool to provide customers a look around their workplace. Netscape was known for this back in its heyday. The Webcams located on these companies' premises were obviously authorized by upper management. A look inside a facility can be a huge benefit if your job boils down to a physical assessment. Second, it's not all that uncommon for a Webcam to be placed outside a facility, as shown in Figure 8.8. This type of cam is a boon for a physical assessment. Also, don't forget that what an employee does at work doesn't necessarily reflect what he does on his own time. If you locate an employee's personal Web space, there's a fair chance that these types of devices will exist.

FIGURE 8.8

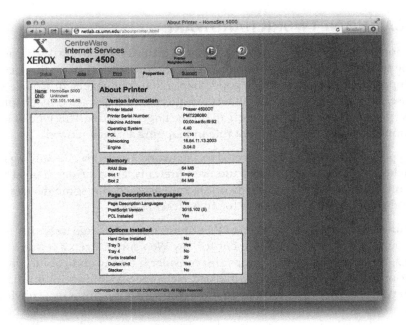

FIGURE 8.9

Most network printers manufactured these days have some sort of Web-based interface installed. If these devices (or even the documentation or drivers supplied with these devices) are linked from a Web page, various Google queries can be used to locate them.

Once located, network printers can provide an attacker with a wealth of information. As shown in Figure 8.9, it is very common for a network printer to list details about the surrounding network, naming conventions, and more. Many devices located through a Google search are still running a default, insecure configuration with no username or password needed to control the device. In a worst-case scenario, attackers can view print jobs and even coerce these printers to store files or even send network commands.

SUMMARY

Attackers use Google for a variety of reasons. An attacker might have access to an exploit for a particular version of Web software and may be on the prowl for vulnerable targets. Other times the attacker might have decided on a target and is using Google to locate information about other devices on the network. In some cases, an attacker could simply be looking for Web devices that are poorly configured with default pages and programs, indicating that the security around the device is soft.

Directory listings provide information about the software versions in use on a device. Server and application error messages can provide a wealth of information to an attacker and are perhaps the most underestimated of all information-gathering techniques. Default pages, programs, and documentation not only can be used to profile a target, but they serve as an indicator that the server is somewhat neglected and perhaps vulnerable to exploitation. Login portals, while serving as the "front door" of a Web server for regular users, can be used to profile a target, used to locate more information about services and procedures in use, and used as a virtual magnet for attackers armed with matching exploits. In some cases, login portals are set up by administrators to allow remote access to a server or network. This type of login portal, if compromised, can provide an entry point for an intruder as well.

Google can be used to locate or augment Web-based networking tools like NQT, which enables remote execution of various network-querying applications. Using creative queries, Google may even locate Web-enabled network devices in use by the target or output from network statistical packages. Whatever your goal during a network-based assessment, there's a good chance Google can be used to augment your existing tools and techniques.

CHAPTER 9

Usernames, Passwords, and Secret Stuff, Oh My!

INTRODUCTION

This chapter is not about finding sensitive data during an assessment as much as it is about what the "bad guys" might do to troll for the data. The examples presented in this chapter generally represent the lowest-hanging fruit on the security tree. Hackers target this information on a daily basis. To protect against this type of attacker, we need to be fairly candid about the worst-case possibilities. We won't be *overly* candid, however. We don't want to give the bad guys any ideas they don't already have.

We start by looking at some queries that can be used to uncover usernames, the less important half of most authentication systems. The value of a username is often overlooked, but as we've already discussed, an entire multimillion-dollar security system can be shattered through skillful crafting of even the smallest, most innocuous bit of information.

Next, we will take a look at queries that are designed to uncover passwords. Some of the queries we look at reveal encrypted or encoded passwords, which will take a bit of work on the part of an attacker to use to his or her advantage. We also take a look at queries that can uncover *cleartext* passwords. These queries are some of the most dangerous in the hands of even the most novice attacker. What could make an attack easier than handing a username and cleartext password to an attacker?

We wrap up this chapter by discussing the *very real* possibility of uncovering highly sensitive data such as credit card information and information used to commit identity theft, such as Social Security numbers. Our goal here is to explore ways of protecting against this very real threat. To that end, we don't go into details about uncovering financial information and the like. If you're a "dark side" hacker, you'll need to figure these things out on your own, or make the wise decision to turn to the light side of the force.

SEARCHING FOR USERNAMES

Most authentication mechanisms use a username and password to protect information. To get through the "front door" of this type of protection, you'll need to determine usernames as well as passwords. Usernames also can be used for social engineering efforts, as we discussed earlier.

Many methods can be used to determine usernames. In Chapter 4, we explored ways of gathering usernames via database error messages. In Chapter 8, we explored Web server and application error messages that can reveal various kinds of information, including usernames. These indirect methods of locating usernames are helpful, but an attacker could target a usernames directory with a simple query like *"your username is"*. This phrase can locate help pages that describe the username creation process.

An attacker could use this information to postulate a username based on information gleaned from other sources, such as Google Groups posts or phone listings. The usernames could then be recycled into various other phases of the attack, such as a worm-based spam campaign or a social-engineering attempt. An attacker can gather usernames from a variety of sources.

In some cases, usernames can be gathered from Web-based statistical programs that check Web activity. The Webalizer program shows all sorts of information about a Web server's usage. Output files for the Webalizer program can be located with a query such as *+intext:webalizer +intext:"Total Usernames" +intext:"Usage Statistics for"*. Among the information displayed is the username that was used to connect to the Web server. In some cases, however, the usernames displayed are not valid or current, but the "Visits" column lists the number of times a user account was used during the capture period. This enables an attacker to easily determine which accounts are more likely to be valid.

The Windows registry holds all sorts of authentication information, including usernames and passwords. Though it is unlikely (and fairly uncommon) to locate live, exported Windows registry files on the Web, at the time of this writing there are nearly 200 hits on the query *filetype:reg HKEY_CURRENT_USER username*, which locates Windows registry files that contain the word *username* and in some cases passwords.

Remember that there are several ways to search for a known filename. One way relies on locating the file in a directory listing, like *intitle:index.of install. log*. Another, often better, method relies on the *filetype* operator, as in *filetype:log inurl:install.log*. Directory listings are not all that common. Google will crawl a link to a file in a directory listing, meaning that the *filetype* method will find *both* directory listing entries as well as files crawled in other ways.

As any talented attacker or security person will tell you, it's rare to get information served to you on a silver platter. Most decent finds take a bit of persistence,

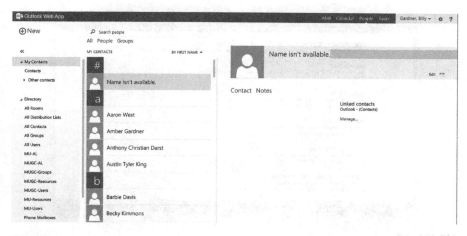

FIGURE 9.1

creativity, intelligence, and just a bit of good luck. For example, consider the Microsoft Outlook Web Access portal, which can be located with a query like *inurl:root.asp?acs = anon*. There are few hits for this query, even though there lots of sites run the Microsoft Web-based mail portal. Regardless of how you might locate a site running this email gateway, it's not uncommon for the site to host a public directory (denoted "Find Names," by default), as shown in Figure 9.1.

The public directory allows access to a search page that can be used to find users by name. In most cases, wildcard searching is not allowed, meaning that a search for * will not return a list of all users, as might be expected. Entering a search for a space is an interesting idea; since most user descriptions contain a space, but most large directories will return an error message reading "This query would return too many addresses!" Applying a bit of creativity, an attacker could begin searching for individual common letters, such as the "Wheel of Fortune letters" *R, S, T, L, N, and E.* Eventually one of these searches will most likely reveal a list of user information.

Once a list of user information is returned, the attacker can then recycle the search with words contained in the user list, searching for the words *Voyager, Freshmen,* or *Campus,* for example. Those results can then be recycled, eventually resulting in a nearly complete list of user information.

SEARCHING FOR PASSWORDS

Password data, one of the "Holy Grails" during a penetration test, should be protected. Unfortunately, many examples of Google queries can be used to locate passwords on the Web.

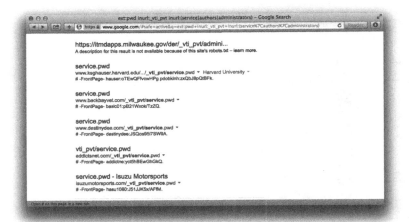

FIGURE 9.2

In most cases, passwords discovered on the Web are either encrypted or encoded in some way. In most cases, these passwords can be fed into a password cracker such as John the Ripper from www.openwall.com/john to produce plaintext passwords that can be used in an attack. Figure 9.2 shows the results of the search ext:pwd inurl:_vti_pvt inurl:(Service | authors | administrators), which combines a search for some common Microsoft FrontPage support files. While Microsoft FrontPage is no longer supported by Microsoft it can still be found in use around. Note that live, exported Windows registry files are not very common, but it's not uncommon for an attacker to target a site simply because of one exceptionally insecure file. It's also possible for a Google query to uncover cleartext passwords. These passwords can be used as is, without having to employ a password-cracking utility. In these extreme cases, the only challenge is determining the username as well as the host on which the password can be used. As shown in Figure 9.3, certain queries will locate all the following information: usernames, cleartext passwords, and the host that uses that authentication!

There is no magic query for locating passwords, but during an assessment, remember that the simplest queries directed at a site can have amazing results, as we discussed in Chapter 7. For example, a query like "Your password" forgot would locate pages that provide a forgotten password recovery mechanism. The information from this type of query can be used to formulate any number of attacks against a password. As always, effective social engineering is a terrific nontechnical solution to "forgotten" passwords.

Another generic search for password information, intext:(password | passcode | pass) intext:(username | userid | user), combines common words for passwords

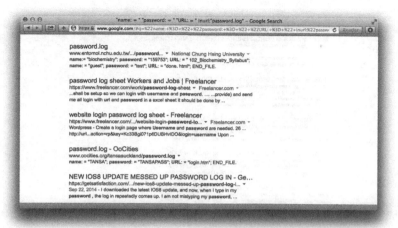

FIGURE 9.3

and user IDs into one query. This query returns a lot of results, but the vast majority of the top hits refer to pages that list forgotten password information, including either links or contact information.

Using Google's translate feature, found at http://translate.google.com/translate_t, we could also create multilingual password searches. Note that the terms username and userid in most languages translate to username and userid, respectively.

SEARCHING FOR CREDIT CARD NUMBERS, SOCIAL SECURITY NUMBERS, AND MORE

Most people have heard news stories about Web hackers making off with customer credit card information. With so many fly-by night retailers popping up on the Internet, it's no wonder that credit card fraud is so prolific. These mom-and-pop retailers are not the only ones successfully compromised by hackers. Corporate giants by the hundreds have had financial database compromises over the years, victims of sometimes very technical, highly focused attackers.

What might surprise you is that it doesn't take a rocket scientist to uncover live credit card numbers on the Internet as seen in Figure 9.4. Thanks to search engines like Google, everything from credit information to banking data or supersensitive classified government documents can be found on the Web.

This document, found using Google, lists hundreds and hundreds of credit card numbers (including expiration date and card validation numbers) as well as the owners' names, addresses, and phone numbers. This particular document also included phone card (calling card) numbers. In most cases, pages

FIGURE 9.4

that contain these numbers are not "leaked" from online retailers or e-commerce sites but rather are most likely the fruits of a scam known as *phishing*, in which users are solicited via telephone or email for personal information. Several Web sites, including MillerSmiles.co.uk, document these scams and hoaxes. Figure 9.5 shows a screenshot of a popular eBay phishing scam that encourages users to update their eBay profile information.

Once a user fills out this form, all the information is sent via email to the attacker, who can use it for just about anything. Sometimes this data is stored on a Web server used by the attacker. In some cases I've seen online "phishing investigators" post reports which link to the phisher's cache of pilfered

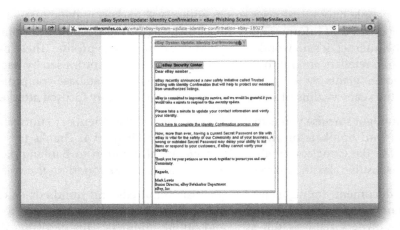

FIGURE 9.5

personal data. When a search engine crawls those links, all that personal data is suddenly available to even the most amateur Google hacker.

SOCIAL SECURITY NUMBERS

Attackers can use similar techniques to home in on Social Security numbers (SSNs) and other sensitive data. For a variety of reasons, SSNs might appear online – for example, educational facilities are notorious for using an SSN as a student ID, then posting grades to a public Web site with the "student ID" displayed next to the grade. A creative attacker can do quite a bit with just an SSN, but in many cases it helps to also have a name associated with that SSN. Again, educational facilities have been found exposing this information via Excel spreadsheets listing student's names, grades, and SSNs, despite the fact that the student ID number is often used to help protect the privacy of the student! Although I've never revealed how to locate SSN's, several media outlets have done just that – irresponsibly posting the search details online. Although the blame lies with the sites that are leaking this information, in my opinion it's still not right to draw attention to how exactly the information can be located.

PERSONAL FINANCIAL DATA

In some cases, phishing scams are responsible for publicizing personal information; in other cases, hackers attacking online retails are to blame for this breach of privacy. Sadly, there are many instances where an individual is *personally* responsible for his own lack of privacy. Such is the case with personal financial information. With the explosion of personal computers in today's society, users have literally *hundreds* of personal finance programs to choose from. Many of these programs create data files with specific file extensions that can be searched with Google. It's hard to imagine why anyone would post personal financial information to a public Web site (which subsequently gets crawled by Google), but it must happen quite a bit, judging by the number of hits for program files generated by Quicken and Microsoft Money, for example. Although it would be somewhat irresponsible to provide queries here that would unearth personal financial data, it's important to understand the types of data that could potentially be uncovered by an attacker.

SEARCHING FOR OTHER JUICY INFO

As we've seen, Google can be used to locate all sorts of sensitive information. In this section we take a look at some of the data that Google can find that's harder to categorize. From address books to chat log files and network vulnerability reports, there's no shortage of sensitive data online.

Some of this information is fairly benign – for example, MSN Messenger contact list files that can be found with a query like *filetype:ctt messenger*, or AOL Instant Messenger (AIM) buddy lists that can be located with a query such as *filetype:blt blt +intext:screenname*.

This screen shows a list of "buddies," or acquaintances an individual has entered into his or her AIM client. An attacker often uses personal information like this in a social-engineering attack, attempting to convince the target that they are a friend or an acquaintance. This practice is akin to pilfering a Rolodex or address book from a target. For a seasoned attacker, information like this can lead to a successful compromise. However, in some cases, data found with a Google query reveals sensitive security-related information that even the most novice attacker could use to compromise a system.

For example, consider the output of the Nessus security scanner available from www.nessus.org. This excellent open-source tool conducts a series of security tests against a target, reporting on any potential vulnerability. The report generated by Nessus can then be used as a guide to help system administrators lock down any affected systems. An attacker could also use a report like this to uncover a target's potential vulnerabilities. Using a Google query such as *"This file was generated by Nessus"*, an attacker could locate reports generated by the Nessus tool. This report lists the IP address of each tested machine as well as the ports opened and any vulnerabilities that were detected.

In most cases, reports found in this manner are samples, or test reports, but in a few cases, the reports are live and the tested systems *are*, in fact, exploitable as listed. One can only hope that the reported systems are honeypots – machines created for the sole purpose of luring and tracing the activities of hackers. In the next chapter, we'll talk more about "document-grinding" techniques, which are also useful for digging up this type of information. This chapter focused on locating the information based on the name of the file, whereas the next chapter focuses on the actual *content* of a document rather than the name.

SUMMARY

Make no mistake – there's sensitive data on the Web, and Google can find it. There's hardly any limit to the scope of information that can be located, if only you can figure out the right query. From usernames to passwords, credit card and Social Security numbers, and personal financial information, it's all out there. As a purveyor of the "dark arts," you can relish in the stupidity of others, but as a professional tasked with securing a customer's site from this dangerous form of information leakage, you could be overwhelmed by the sheer scale of your defensive duties.

As droll as it might sound, a solid, enforced security policy is a great way to keep sensitive data from leaking to the Web. If users understand the risks associated with information leakage and understand the penalties that come with violating policy, they will be more willing to cooperate in what should be a security partnership.

In the meantime, it certainly doesn't hurt to understand the tactics an adversary might employ in attacking a Web server. One thing that should become clear as you read this book is that any attacker has an overwhelming number of files to go after. One way to prevent dangerous Web information leakage is by denying requests for unknown file types. Whether your Web server normally serves up CFM, ASP, PHP, or HTML, it's infinitely easier to manage what *should* be served by the Web server instead of focusing on what should *not* be served. Adjust your servers or your border protection devices to allow only specific content or file types.

CHAPTER 10

Hacking Google Services

CALENDAR

Google Calendar is powerful calendar management application, which supports features like calendar sharing, creation of invitations, search and calendar publishing. The service is also integrated with Google Mail (GMail) and can be accessed via a Mobile device. All in all, Google Calendar is very useful addition to our day-to-day work.

Calendar sharing in particular is a very useful feature since individual users can maintain event lists and calendars to which others may be interested in as well. Usually in order to share a calendar you have to explicitly do so from the calendar management interface.

Once the calendar is shared, everyone will be able to look at it or even subscribe to the events that are inside. This can be done via the Calendar application or any RSS feed reader.

As a security expert, these shared calendars are especially interesting. Very often, even when performing the most basic searches, it is entirely possible to stumble across sensitive information that can be used for malicious purposes. For example, logging into Calendar and searching for the term "password" returns many results.

As you can see, there are several calendar entries that meet our search criteria. Among them, there are a few that are quite interesting and worth our attention. Another interesting query that brings a lot of juicy information is "passcode", as shown in Figure 10.1.

Figure 10.1 reveals several scheduled telephone conferences. Notice that the conference phone number and access code are also listed. An attacker could easily join the telephone conference at the scheduled time and silently eavesdrop on the conference. Mission accomplished. There is a lot attackers can learn from the conversation, like corporate secrets, technical details about systems in operations, etc.

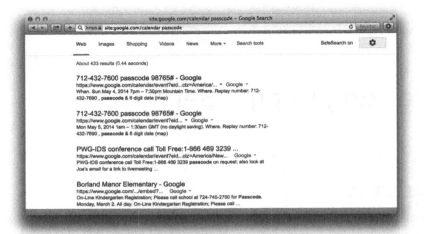

FIGURE 10.1

Of course we can try variations of the above queries and even space them up with more keywords so we can get a better picture. For example the query *"username password"* returns results about people who may store sensitive login information within their calendar.

This is just the beginning though, how about looking for birthdays, pet's names, etc. As you probably know, a lot of password reminder facilities have a secret question. The secrets answer is usually something that we choose from our daily life so there is no chance that we can forget. However, the Calendar application may also contain our daily activities. When we mash both, we might be able to crack into the targeted user account by simply reading their calendar.

There are many different ways; the Calendar service can be abused. The main and most important security consideration that we, as users, need to make is whether the information that is enclosed within the Google's shiny event cells is sensitive and can be used to harm us.

SIGNALING ALERTS

Very often we need to track changes in Google's result set. For example, let's say that we want to monitor a certain site for vulnerabilities. How can we do that? We can simply run scanners every once in a while but this is a noisy exercise and will definitely take loads of time. Instead, being dedicated Google hackers, we can use Google itself and use a few powerful Google dorks to locate the things that we are interested in without the need for automated scanning software. Then we can setup a *cron* task to monitor the results returned by Google and when a change is detected email us the result.

Then again, we could simply use Google Alerts. Google Alerts is a powerful system that detects when a query's result set changes. The system can be modified to send updates once a day, once a week, or as they happen. Keep in mind that only the first 10 entries (the first page) are taken into consideration. Nevertheless, the Alert system does a good job when optimized.

This is a great tool, but it can be used for more interesting purposes. Let's say that we know that a target is using MsSQL as database backend. We could use Google alerts to poll the target, searching for error messages as they pop up. That search might look something like this:

"[SQL Server Driver][SQL Server]Line 1: Incorrect syntax near" -forum -thread -showthread **site:example.com**

For the type of alert select **Web**, usually default option. Select the frequency of the alert, and your email address and click **Create Alert**.

Notice that the query that we use for this alert is domain restricted (**site:example. com**). Also pay attention to the actual Google dork. Obviously we look for messages that look like generated failures in the SQL queries sent to backend. These types of messages are sign for SQL Injection vulnerable resources.

A malicious user can use this service to alert whenever a vulnerability or interesting message appears on a target site. This is very low profile, and does not alert the target; the transaction happens between the user and Google. An attacker could even enter alerts for every entry in the Google Hacking Database. Although this would be overkill, some of the entries in the database reveal extremely sensitive information, which could be harvested with very little further effort.

GOOGLE CO-OP

Google Co-op (www.google.com/coop) is a powerful service that allows you to create powerful custom search engines. You do not need to be registered Google user in order to *use* the service but if you want to create an engine, it is required. In the following section, we'll guide you through some of the most interesting features of this service and we'll show you how to create your own search engines.

Let's start with the simplest of search engines. Browse the Google Co-op page and click **Create a Custom Search Engine**, or simply browse to www.google. com/coop/cse. From the Custom Engine configuration page we need to define the characteristics we need.

First enter a search engine name. We'll call ours the "Google Hacking Database Search." Enter a description and some basic search keywords, both of which are optional. The keywords are primarily used by Google to find the most relevant results. This means that our query will be mingled with these keywords. For now, we'll leave this alone. Moving forward, to the field titled *What do you want to search*, we will define the scope of the search queries. For this example, we are going to use the default option entitled *Only sites that I select*.

Now, the interesting part, we need to supply the URLs Google will look into when performing the queries. Since our search engine will do stuff around the Google Hacking Database located at https://www.exploit-db.com/google-hacking-database/, we'll simply drop that URL into this field. We'll customize this entry option further with the use of wildcards, in order to search URLs that match a specific syntax. Here are a few examples taken from Co-op's documentation:

www.mysite.com/mypage.html - look for information within mypage.html part of the

www.mysite.com domain

www.mysite.com/* - look for information within the entire context of

www.mysite.com

www.mysite.com/*about* - look for information within URLs from

www.mysite.com that

has the about keyword

*.mydomain.com - look for information within sub-domains of mysite.com.

The rest of the options from the Co-op Custom engine creation page are irrelevant at this point. Agree to Google's terms of service and click on the next button.

No we'll test how the search engine works. Type a few queries like "index" or "secret," and you'll see some sample results. If everything works as expected, click *finish*, and the custom search engine will be displayed.

GOOGLE'S CUSTOM SEARCH ENGINE

The GNUCITIZEN group http://www.gnucitizen.org has discovered that Google's Custom Search Engine platform can be used for many other useful things such as fingerprinting and enumerating hidden Web servers. It is well known fact that not all Web resources are exposed to the Internet. We call that part of the network the hidden Web. By using Custom Search Engines we can recover them and enumerate their content. Among the gathered information, we may find Intranet interfaces, administrative panels and other types of sensitive information.

CHAPTER 11

Hacking Google Showcase

INTRODUCTION

A self-respecting Google hacker spends hours trolling the Internet for juicy stuff. Firing off search after search, they thrive on the thrill of finding clean, mean, streamlined queries and get a real rush from sharing those queries and trading screenshots of their findings. I know because I've seen it with my own eyes. As the founder of the Google Hacking Database (GHDB) and the Search engine hacking forums at http://johnny.ihackstuff.com, I am constantly amazed at what the Google hacking community comes up with. It turns out the rumors are true – creative Google searches can reveal medical, financial, proprietary and even classified information. Despite government edicts, regulation, and protection acts like HIPPA and the constant barking of security watchdogs, this problem still persists. Stuff still makes it out onto the Web, and Google hackers snatch it right up.

In my quest to put a spotlight on the threat, I began speaking on the topic of Google hacking at security conferences like Blackhat and Defcon. In addition, I was approached to write my first book, the first edition of the book that you're holding. After months of writing, I assumed our cause would finally catch the eye of the community at large and that change would be on the horizon. I just knew people would be talking about Google hacking and that awareness about the problem would increase.

Google Hacking, first edition, has made a difference. But nothing made waves like the "Google Hacking Showcase," the fun part of my infamous Google hacking conference talks. The showcase wasn't a big deal to me – it consisted of nothing more than screenshots of wild Google hacks I had witnessed. Borrowing from the pool of interesting Google queries I had created, along with scores of queries from the community; I snagged screenshots and presented them one at a time, making smarmy comments along the way. Every time I presented the showcase, I managed to whip the audience into a frenzy of laughter at the absurd effectiveness of a hacker armed only with a browser and a search engine. It was fun, and it was effective. People talked about those screenshots for months

175

after each talk. They were, after all, the fruits of a Google hacker's labor. Those photos represented the white-hot center of the Google hacking threat.

It made sense then to include the showcase in this edition of *Google Hacking*. In keeping with the original format of the showcase, this chapter will be heavy on photos and light on gab because the photos speak for themselves. Some of the screenshots in this chapter are dated, and some no longer exist on the Web, but this is great news. It means that somewhere in the world, someone (perhaps inadvertently) graduated from the level of *googledork* and has taken a step closer to a better security posture. Regardless, I left in many outdated photos as a stark reminder to those charged with protecting online resources. They serve as proof that this threat is pervasive – it can happen to anyone, and history has shown that it has happened to just about everyone.

So without further ado, enjoy this print version of the Google Hacking Showcase, brought to you by Johnny Long and the contributions of the Google Hacking community.

GEEK STUFF

This section is about computer stuff. It's about technical stuff, the stuff of geeks. We will take a look at some of the more interesting technical finds uncovered by Google hackers. We'll begin by looking at various utilities that really have no business being online, unless of course your goal is to aid hackers. Then we'll look at open network devices and open applications, neither of which requires any real hacking to gain access to.

Utilities

Any self-respecting hacker has a war chest of tools at his disposal, but the thing that's interesting about the tools in this section is that they are online – they run on a Web server and allow an attacker to effectively bounce his reconnaissance efforts off of that hosting Web server. To make matters worse, these application-hosting servers were each located with clever Google queries. We'll begin with the handy PHP script shown in Figure 11.1 That allows a Web visitor to *ping* any target on the Internet. A *ping* isn't necessarily a bad thing, but why offer the service to anonymous visitors?

Unlike the *ping* tool, the *finger* tool has been out of commission for quite a long time. This annoying service allowed attackers to query users on a UNIX machine, allowing enumeration of all sorts of information such as user connect times, home directory, full name and more. Enter the *finger* CGI script, an awkward attempt to "webify" this irritating service. As shown in Figure 11.2, a well-placed Google query locates installations of this script, providing Web visitors with a *finger* client that allows them to query the service on remote machines.

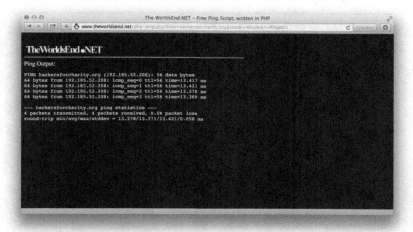

FIGURE 11.1

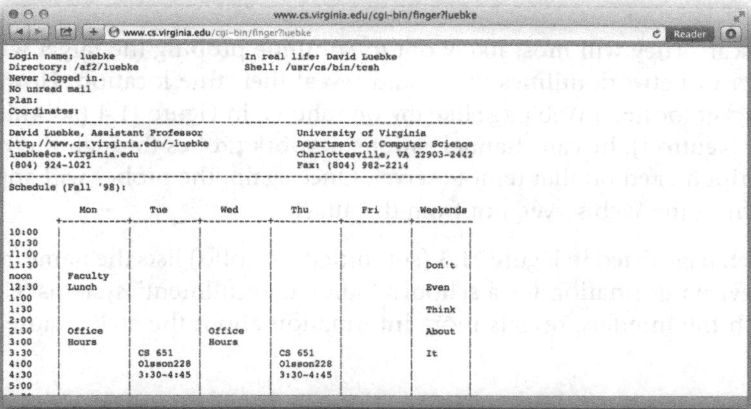

FIGURE 11.2

Pings and *finger* lookups are relatively benign; most system administrators won't even notice them traversing their networks. *Portscans*, on the other hand, are hardly ever considered benign, and a paranoid administrator (or piece of defense software) will take note of the source of a portscan. Although most modern portscanners provide options, which allow for covert operation, a little Google hacking can go a long way. Figure 11.3 reveals a Google search submitted by Jimmy Neutron that locates sites that will allow a Web visitor to portscan a target.

Remember, scans performed in this way will originate from the Web server, not from the attacker. Even the most paranoid system administrator will struggle to trace a scan launched in this way. Of course, most attackers won't stop at

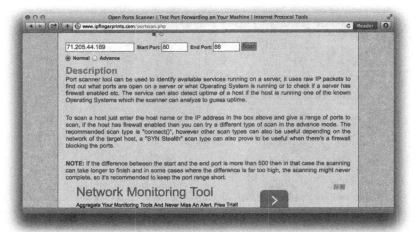

FIGURE 11.3

a portscan. They will most likely opt to continue probing the target with any number of network utilities that could reveal their true location. However, if an attacker locates a Web page like the one shown in Figure 11.4 (submitted by Jimmy Neutron), he can channel various network probes through the *WebUtil* Perl script hosted on that remote server. Once again, the probes will appear to come from the Web server, not from the attacker.

The Web page listed in Figure 11.5 (submitted by Golfo) lists the name, address and device information for a school's "student enrollment" systems. Clicking through the interface reveals more information about the architecture of the

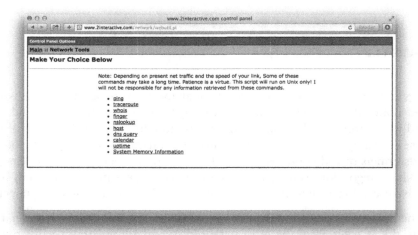

FIGURE 11.4

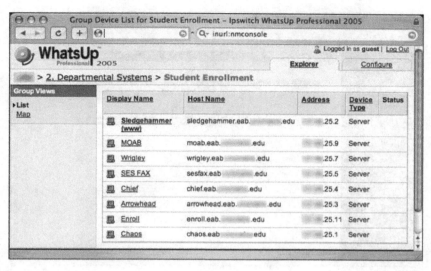

FIGURE 11.5

network, and the devices connected to it. Consolidated into one easy-to-read interface and located with a Google search, this page makes short work of an attacker's reconnaissance run.

OPEN NETWORK DEVICES

Why hack into a network server or device when you can just point and click your way into an *open* network device? Management devices, like the one submitted by Jimmy Neutron in Figure 11.6, often list all sorts of information about a variety of devices.

When m00d submitted the query shown in Figure 11.7, I honestly didn't think much of it. The SpeedStream router is a decidedly lightweight device installed by home users, but I was startled to find them sitting wide-open on the Internet. I personally like the button in the point-to-point summary listing. Who do you want to disconnect today?

Belkin is a household name in home network gear. With their easy-to-use Web-based administrative interfaces, it makes sense that eventually pages like the one in Figure 11.8 would get crawled by Google. Even without login credentials, this page reveals a ton of information that could be interesting to a potential attacker. I got a real laugh out of the *Features* section of the page. The firewall is enabled, but the wireless interface is wide open and unencrypted. As a hacker with a social conscience, my first instinct is to enable

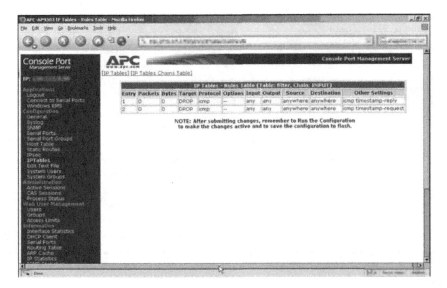

FIGURE 11.6

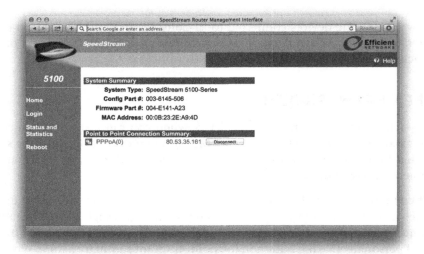

FIGURE 11.7

encryption on this access point – in an attempt to protect this poor home user from themselves.

Milkman brings us the query shown in Figure 11.9, which digs up the configuration interface for Smoothwall personal firewalls. There's something just wrong about Google hacking someone's firewall.

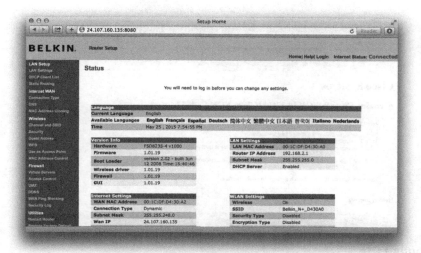

FIGURE 11.8

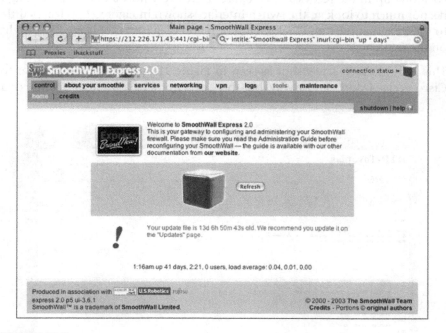

FIGURE 11.9

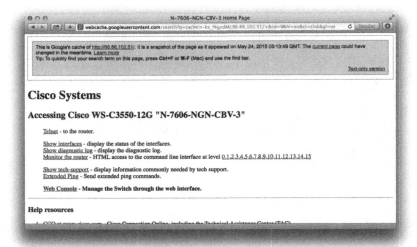

FIGURE 11.10

As Jimmy Neutron reveals in the next two figures, even big-name gear like Cisco shows up in the recesses of Google's cache every now and again. Although it's not much to look at, the switch interface shown in Figure 11.10 leaves little to the imagination – all the configuration and diagnostic tools are listed right on the main page.

This second Cisco screenshot as seen in Figure 11.11 should look familiar to Cisco geeks. I don't know why, but the Cisco nomenclature reminds me of a

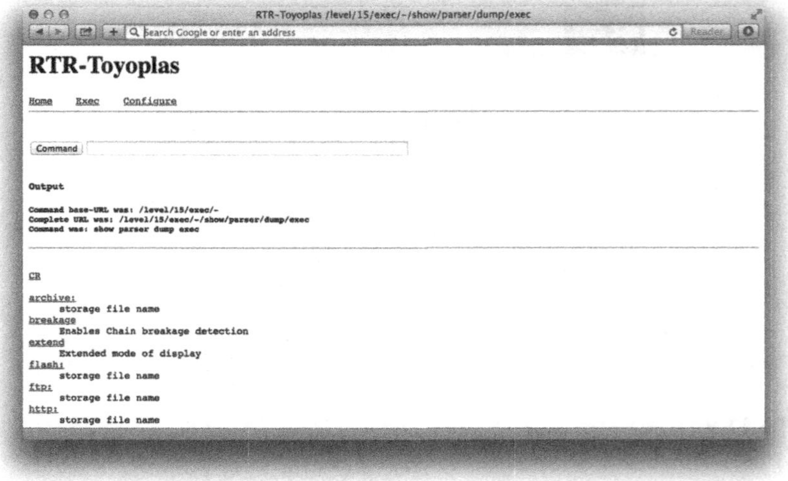

FIGURE 11.11

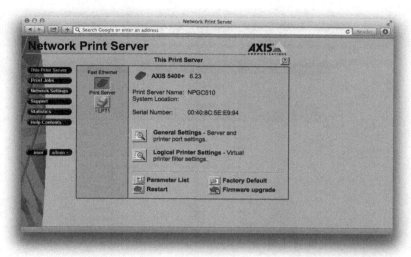

FIGURE 11.12

bad Hollywood flick. I can almost hear the grating voice of an oversynthesized computer beckoning, "Welcome to Level 15."

The search shown in Figure 11.12 (submitted by Murfie) locates interfaces for an Axis network print server. Most printer interfaces are really boring, but this one in particular piqued my interest. First, there's the button named *configuration wizard*, which I'm pretty sure launches a configuration wizard. Then there's the handy link labeled *Print Jobs*, which lists the print jobs. In case you haven't already guessed, Google hacking sometimes leaves little to the imagination.

Printers aren't entirely boring things. Consider the *Web Image Monitor* shown in Figure 11.13. I particularly like the document on *Recent Religion Work*. That's quite an honorable pursuit, except when combined with the document about *Aphrodisiacs*. I really hope the two documents are unrelated. Then again, nothing surprises me these days.

CP has a way of finding Google hacks that make me laugh, and Figure 11.14 is no exception. Yes, this is the Web-based interface to a municipal water fountain.

After watching the water temperature fluctuate for a few intensely boring seconds, it's only logical to click on the *Control* link to see if it's possible to actually control the municipal water fountain. As Figure 11.15 reveals, yes it is possible to remotely control the municipal water fountain.

One bit of advice though – if you happen to bump into one of these, be nice. Don't go rerouting the power into the water storage system. I think that would definitely constitute an act of terrorism.

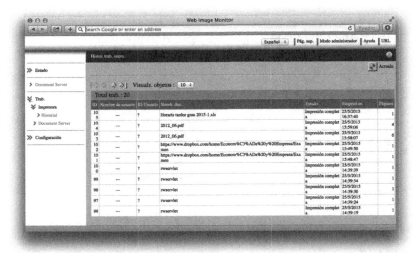

FIGURE 11.13

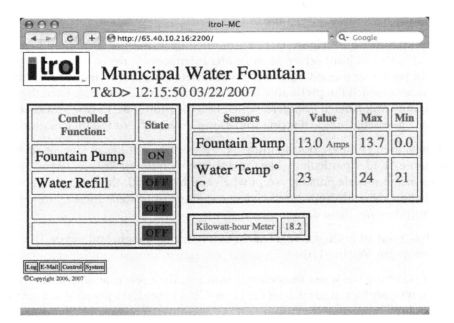

FIGURE 11.14

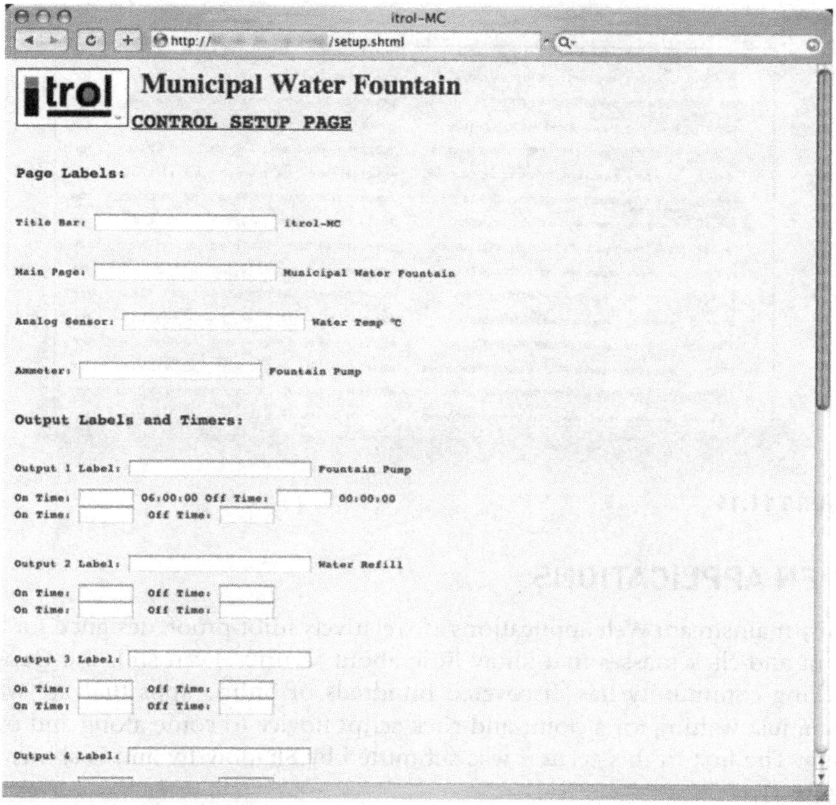

FIGURE 11.15

Moving along to a more traditional network fixture, consider the screenshot captured in Figure 11.16.

Now, I've been in the security business for many years, and I'm not exactly brilliant in any one particular area of the industry. But I do know a little bit about a lot of different things, and one thing I know for sure is that security products are designed to protect stuff. It's the way of things. But when I see something like the log shown in Figure 11.16, I get all confused. See, this is a Web-based interface for the Snort intrusion detection system. The last time I checked, this data was supposed to be kept away from the eyes of an attacker, but I guess I missed an email or something. Yet, I suppose there's logic to this somewhere. Maybe if the attacker sees his mistakes on a public Web page, he'll be too ashamed to ever hack again, and he'll go on to lead a normal productive life. Then again, maybe he and his hacker buddies will just get a good laugh out of his good fortune. It's hard to tell.

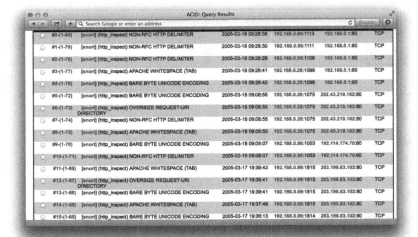

FIGURE 11.16

OPEN APPLICATIONS

Many mainstream Web applications are relatively idiot-proof, designed for the point-and-click masses that know little about security. Even still, the Google hacking community has discovered hundreds of online apps that are wide open, just waiting for a point-and-click script novice to come along and own them. The first in this section was submitted by Shadowsliv and is shown in Figure 11.17.

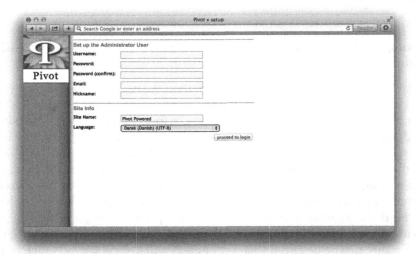

FIGURE 11.17

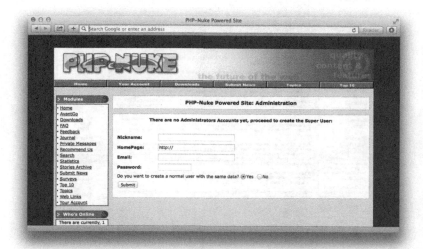

FIGURE 11.18

The bad news is that if a hacker can figure out what to type in those confusing fields, he'll have his very own Pivot Web log. The good news is that most skilled attackers will leave this site alone, figuring that any software left this unprotected *must* be a honey pot. It's really sad that hacking (not *real* hacking mind you) can be reduced to a point-and-click affair, but as Arrested's search reveals in Figure 11.18, owning an entire Web site can be a relatively simple affair.

Sporting one less field than the open Pivot install, this configuration page will create a PHP-Nuke Administrator account, and allow any visitor to start uploading content to the page as if it were their own. Of course, this takes a bit of malicious intent on behalf of the Web visitor. There's no mistaking the fact that he or she is creating an Administrator account on a site that does not belong to them. However, the text of the page in Figure 11.19 is a bit more ambiguous.

The bold text in the middle of the page really cracks me up. I can just imagine somebody's poor Grandma running into this page and reading it aloud. "For security reasons, the best idea is to create the Super User right NOW by clicking HERE." I mean who in their right mind would avoid doing something that was for *security reasons*? For all Grandma knows, she may be saving the world from evil hackers... by hacking into some poor fool's PHP-Nuke install.

And as if owning a Web site isn't cool enough, Figure 11.20 (submitted by Quadster) reveals a phpMyAdmin installation logged in as root, providing unfettered access to a MySQL database.

With a Web site install and an SQL database under his belt, it's a natural progression for a Google hacker to want the ultimate control of a system. VNC

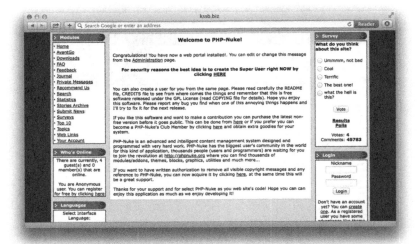

FIGURE 11.19

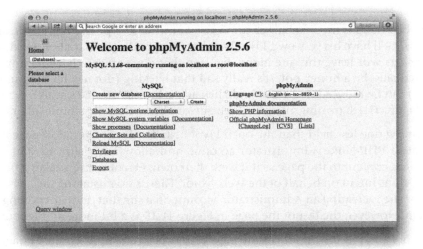

FIGURE 11.20

installations provide remote control of a system's keyboard and mouse. Figure 11.21, submitted by Lester, shows a query that locates RealVNC's Java-based client.

Locating a client is only part of the equation, however. An attacker will still need to know the address, port and (optional) password for a VNC server. As Figure 11.22 reveals, the Java client itself often provides two-thirds of that equation in a handy popup window.

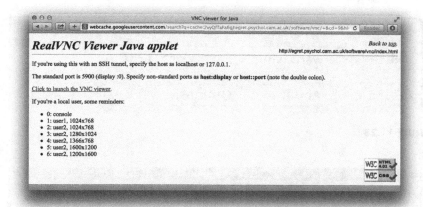

FIGURE 11.21

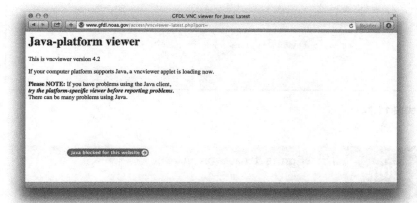

FIGURE 11.22

If the hacker is luckyenough to stumble on a server that's not password protected, he's faced with the daunting task of figuring out which of the four buttons to click in the above connection window. Here's a hint for the script novice looking to make his way in the world: it's not the *Cancel* button.

Of course running without a password is just plain silly. But passwords can be so difficult to remember and software vendors obviously realize this as evidenced by the password prompt shown in Figure 11.23.

Posting the default username/password combination on a login popup is just craziness. Unfortunately it's not an isolated event. Check out Figure 11.24, submitted by Jimmy Neutron. Can you guess the default password?

Graduating to the next level of hacker leetness requires a bit of work. Check out the user screen shown in Figure 11.25, which was submitted by Dan Kaminsky.

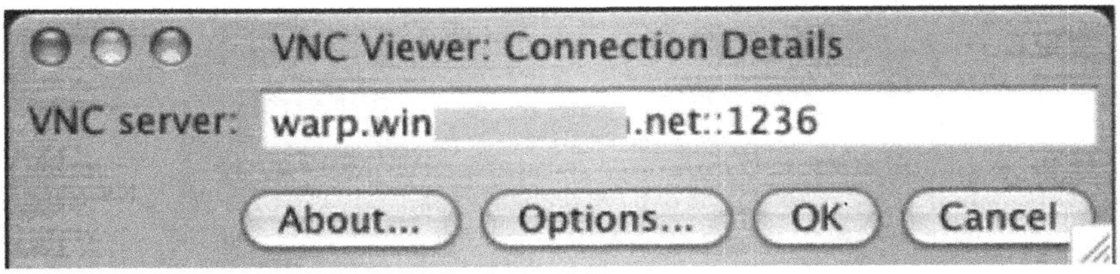

FIGURE 11.23

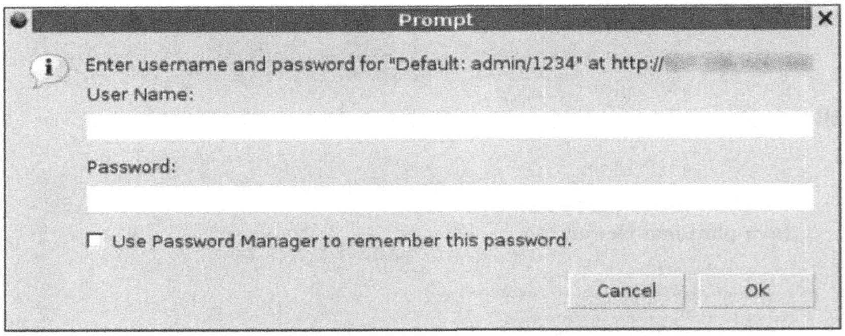

FIGURE 11.24

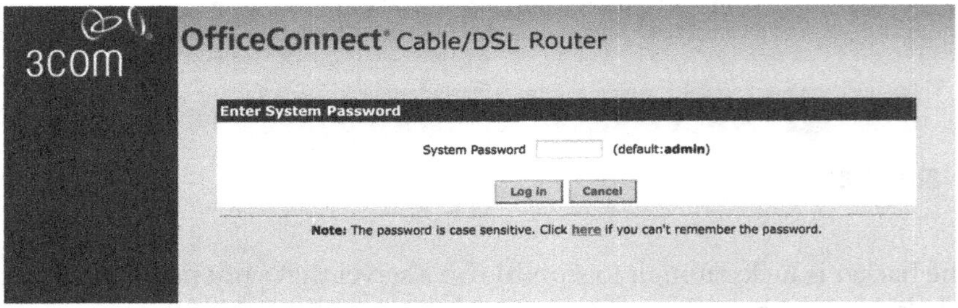

FIGURE 11.25

If you look carefully, you'll notice that the URL contains a special field called *ADMIN*, which is set to *False*. Think like a hacker for a moment and imagine how you might gain administrative access to the page. The spoiler is listed in Figures 11.26 and 11.27.

Check out the shiny new *Exit Administrative Access* button. By Changing the *ADMIN* field to *True*, the application drops us into Administrative access mode. Hacking really is hard, I promise.

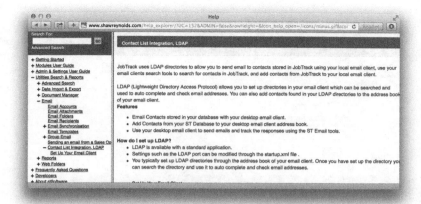

FIGURE 11.26

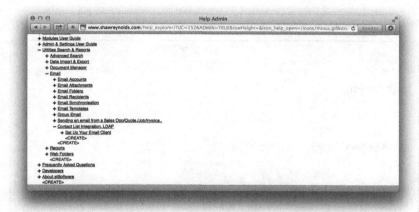

FIGURE 11.27

CAMERAS

I've got to be honest and admit that like printer queries, I'm really sick of Web cam queries. For a while there, every other addition to the GHDB was a Web cam query. Still, some Web cam finds are pretty interesting and worth mentioning in the showcase. I'll start with a cell phone camera dump, submitted by Vipsta as shown in Figures 11.28 and 11.29.

Not only is this an interesting photo of some pretty serious-looking vehicular carnage but the idea that Google trolls camera phone picture sites is interesting. Who knows what kind of blackmail fodder lurks in the world's camera phones. Not that anyone would ever use that kind of information for sensationalistic or economically lucrative purposes. Ahem.

FIGURE 11.28

FIGURE 11.29

Moving on, check out the office-mounted open Web camera submitted by Klouw as shown in Figures 11.30 and 11.31.

This is really an interesting Web cam. Not only does it reveal all the activity in the office, but also it seems especially designed to allow remote shoulder surfing. Hackers had to get out of the house to participate in this classic sport earlier. These days all they have to do is fire off a few Google searches.

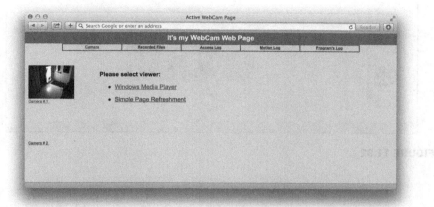

FIGURE 11.30

FIGURE 11.31

FIGURE 11.32

Figure 11.32, however (submitted by JBrashars) is unmistakable. It's definitely a parking lot camera. I'm not sure why, exactly, a camera is pointed at a handicapped parking space, but my guess is that there have been reports of handicapped parking spot abuse. Imagine the joy of being the guard that gets to witness the CIO parking in the spot, leaping out of his convertible and running into the building. Those are the stories of security guard legends.

I can't be the only one that thinks it's insane to put open security camera feeds on the Internet. Of course it happens in Hollywood movies all the time. It seems the first job for the hired hacker is to tap into the video surveillance feeds. But the movies make it look all complicated and technical. I've never once seen a Hollywood hacker use Google to hack the security system. Then again, that wouldn't look nearly as cool as using fiber optic cameras, wire cutters and alligator clips.

Moving on, the search shown in Figure 11.33 (submitted by JBrashars) returns quite a few hits for open Everfocus EDSR applets.

The Everfocus EDSR is a multichannel digital video recording system with a Web-based interface. It's a decent surveillance product, and as such it is password protected by default, as shown in Figure 11.34.

Unfortunately, as revealed by an anonymous contributor, the factory-default administrative username and password provides access to many of these systems, as shown in Figure 11.35.

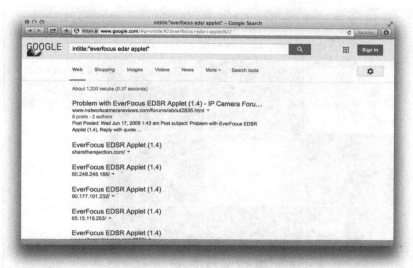

FIGURE 11.33

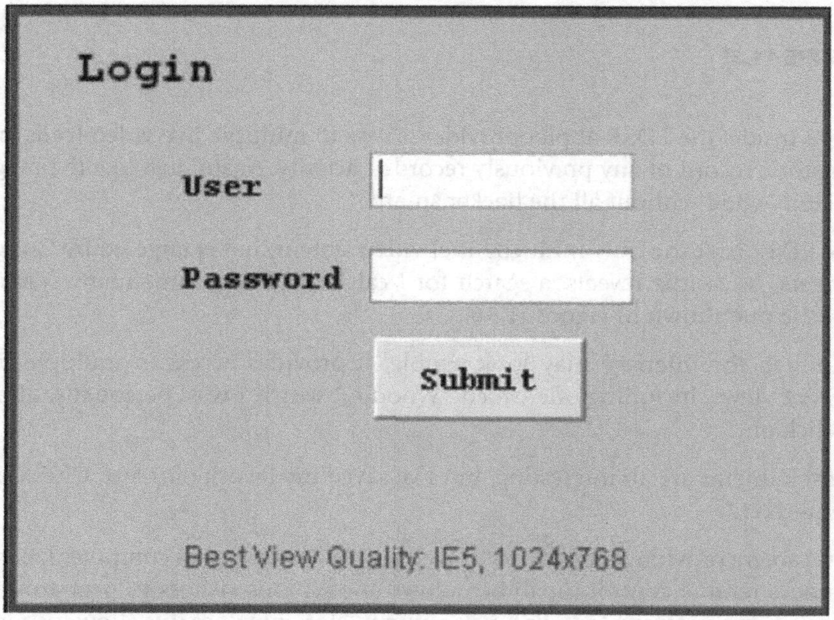

FIGURE 11.34

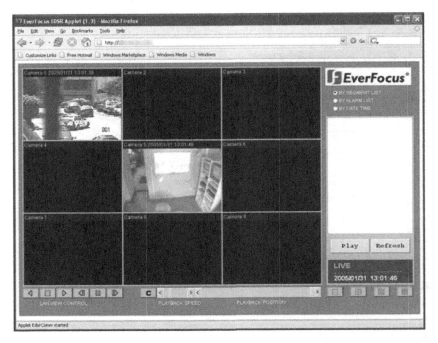

FIGURE 11.35

Once inside, the EDSR applet provides access to multiple live video feeds and a historic record of any previously recorded activity. Again, just like the magic of Hollywood without all the hacker smarts.

The EDSR isn't the only multichannel video system that is targeted by Google hackers. As Murfie reveals, a search for I-catcher CCTV returns many systems like the one shown in Figure 11.36.

Although the interface may look simple, it provides access to multiple live camera views, including one called "Woodie," which I was, personally, afraid to click on.

These cameras are all interesting, but I've saved my favorite for last. Check out Figure 11.37.

This camera provides open access to Web visitors. Located in a computer lab, the camera's remote control capability allows anonymous visitors to peer around, panning and zooming to their hearts content. Not only does this allow for some great shoulder surfing, but also the sticker in the screen capture had me practically falling out of my chair. It lists a username and password for the lab's online FTP server. Stickers listing usernames and passwords are bad enough, but I wonder whose bright idea it was to point an open Web cam at them?

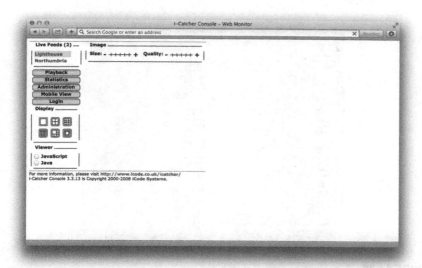

FIGURE 11.36

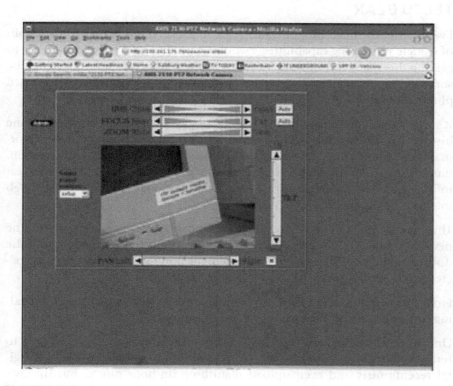

FIGURE 11.37

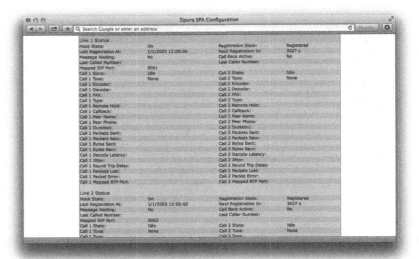

FIGURE 11.38

TELCO GEAR

I've never been much of a phreaker (phone hacker), but thanks to the depth of Google's searching capabilities, I wouldn't need to have much experience to get into this shady line of work. As JBrashar's search reveals in Figure 11.38, the surge of Voice over IP (VOIP) service has resulted in a host of new Web-based phone interfaces.

It's interesting to me that by just using Google, an attacker could get phone history information such as last called number and last caller number. Normally, the Sipura SPA software does a better job of protecting this information, but this particular installation is improperly configured. Other, more technical information can also be uncovered by clicking through the links on the Web interface, as shown in Figure 11.39.

There are so many VOIP devices that it's impossible to cover them all, but the new kid on the VOIP server block is definitely Asterisk. After checking out the documentation for the Asterisk management portal, Jimmy Neutron uncovered the interesting search shown in Figure 11.40.

From this opening, an attacker can make changes to the Asterisk server, including forwarding incoming calls, as shown in Figure 11.41.

Unfortunately, a hacker's fun wouldn't necessarily stop there. It's simple to reroute extensions, monitor or reroute voicemail, enable or disable digital receptionists and even upload disturbing on-hold music. But Jimmy's

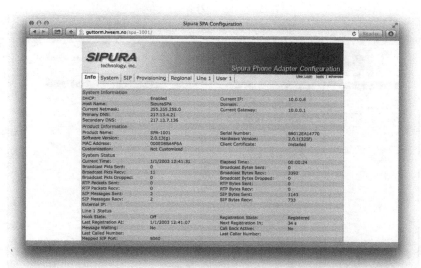

FIGURE 11.39

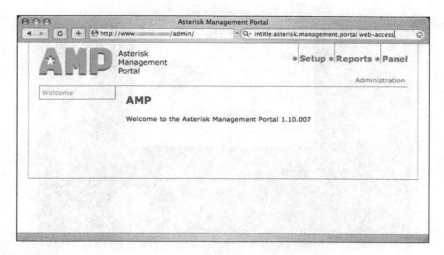

FIGURE 11.40

Asterisk VOIP digging didn't stop there; he later submitted the search shown in Figure 11.42.

This flash-based operator panel provides access to similar capabilities, and once again, the interface was found open to any Internet visitor.

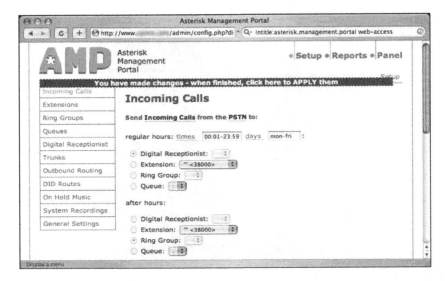

FIGURE 11.41

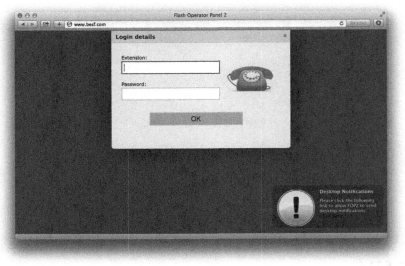

FIGURE 11.42

Moving along, Yeseins serves up the interesting search shown in Figure 11.43, which locates videoconferencing management systems.

This management system allows a Web visitor to connect, disconnect, and monitor conference calls, take snapshots of conference participants, and even change line settings as shown in Figure 11.44.

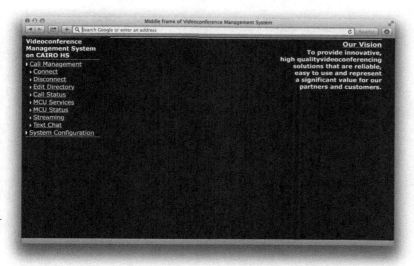

FIGURE 11.43

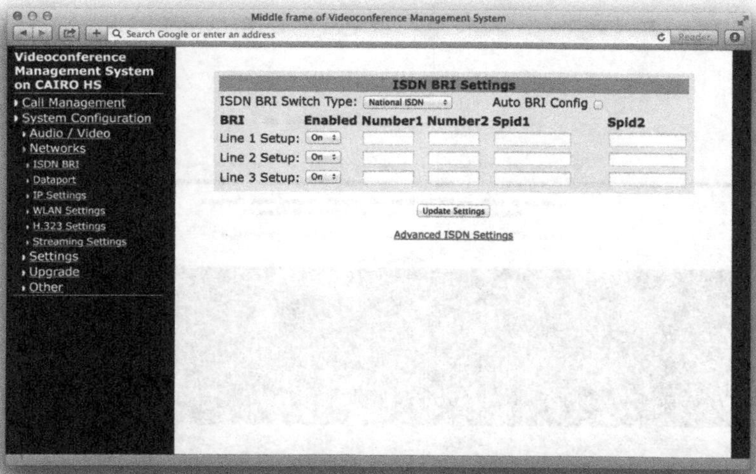

FIGURE 11.44

A malicious hacker could even change the system name and password, locking legitimate administrators out of their own system, as shown in Figure 11.45.

Despite all the new-fangled Web interfaces we've looked at, Google hacking bridges the gap to older systems as well, as shown in Figure 11.46.

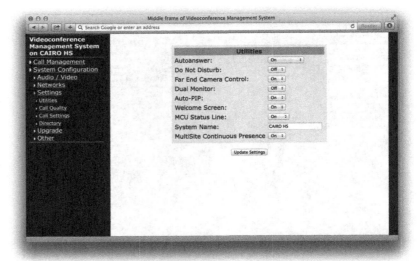

FIGURE 11.45

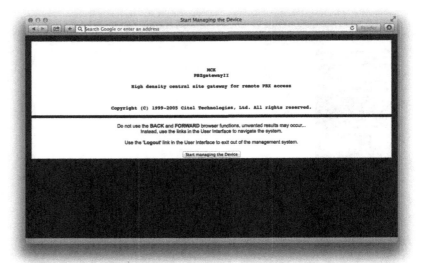

FIGURE 11.46

This front-end was designed to put a new face on an older PBX product, but client security seems to have been an afterthought. Notice that the interface asks the user to "Logout" of the interface, indicating that the user is already logged in. Also, notice that cryptic button labeled *Start Managing the Device*. After firing off a Google search, all a malicious hacker has to do is figure out which button to press. What an unbelievably daunting task.

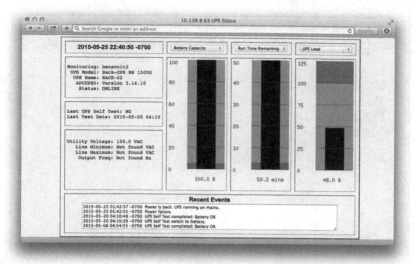

FIGURE 11.47

POWER

I get a lot of raised eyebrows when I talk about using Google to hack power systems. Most people think I'm talking about UPS systems like the one submitted by Yeseins in Figure 11.47.

This is a clever Google query, but it's only an uninterruptible power system (UPS)-monitoring page. This can be amusing, but as Jimmy Neutron shows in Figure 11.48, there are more interesting power hacking opportunities available.

AMX NetLinx systems are designed to allow control of power systems. Figure 11.48 seems to suggest that a Web visitor could control power in a theater, a family room and the master bedroom of a residence. The problem is that the Google search turns up a scarce number of results, most of which are password protected. As an alternative, Jimmy offers the search shown in Figure 11.49.

Although this query results in a long list of password-protected sites, many sites still use the default password, providing access to the control panel shown in Figure 11.50.

This control panel lists power sockets alongside interesting buttons named *Power* and *Restart*, which even the dimmest of hackers will undoubtedly be able to figure out. The problem with this interface is that it's just not much fun. A hacker will definitely get bored flipping unnamed power switches – unless of course he also finds an open Web cam so he can watch the fun. The search shown in Figure 11.51 seems to address this, naming each of the devices for easy reference.

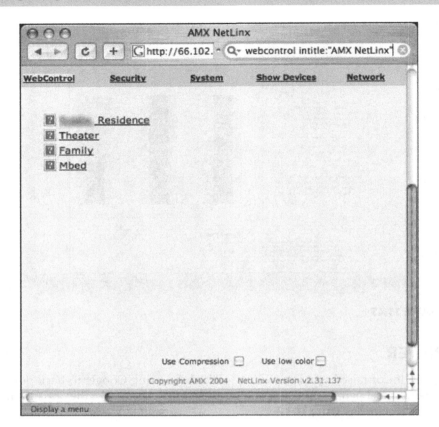

FIGURE 11.48

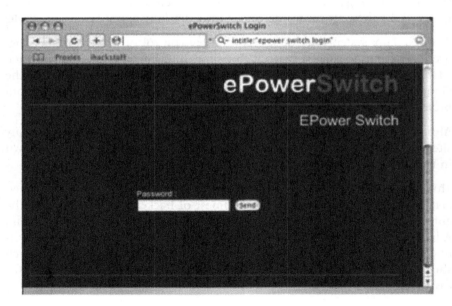

FIGURE 11.49

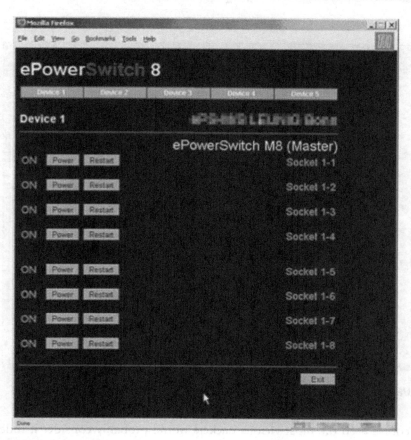

FIGURE 11.50

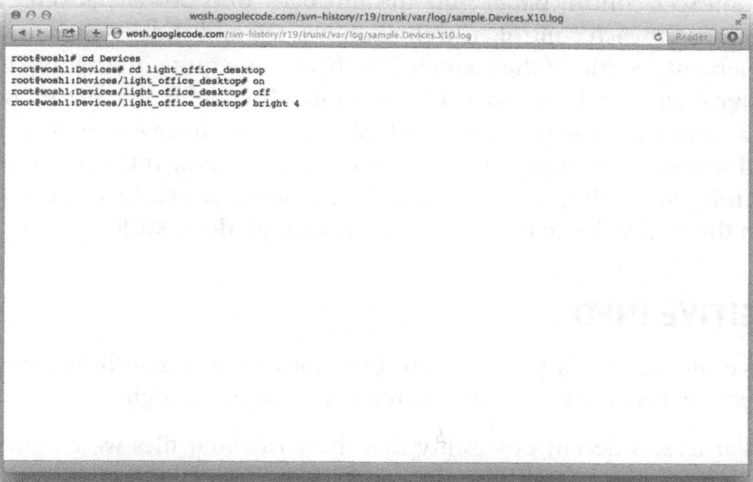

FIGURE 11.51

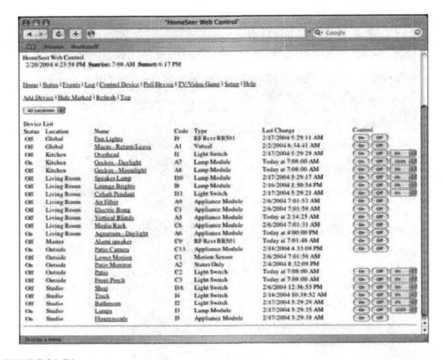

FIGURE 11.52

Of course even the most vicious hackers would probably consider it rude to nail someone's Christmas lights, but no hacker in their right mind could resist the open HomeSeer control panel shown in Figure 11.52.

The HomeSeer control panel puts the fun back into power hacking, listing descriptions for each control, as well as an *On, Off* and slider switch for applicable elements. Some of the elements in this list are quite interesting, including *Lower Motion* and *Bathroom*. The best though is definitely *Electric Bong*. If you're a member of the Secret Service looking to bust the owner of this system, I would suggest a preemptive Google strike before barging into the home. Start by dimming the lights, and then nail the motion sensors. Last but not least, turn on the electric bong in case your other charges don't stick.

SENSITIVE INFO

Sensitive info is such a generic term, but that's what this section includes: a hodgepodge of sensitive info discovered while surfing Google.

There's at least a decent possibility that these calendar files were made public on purpose For starters, the file contains the user's POP email username

FIGURE 11.53

and encoded password. Then there's the issue of his URL history, which contains not only the very respectable *IBM.com*, but also the not-so-respectable *hotchicks.com*, which I'm pretty sure is *NSFW*.

This file lists the contact names and email addresses found in someone's contact list. At best, this file is Spam fodder. There's really no shortage of email address lists, phone number lists and more on the Web, but what's surprising is how many documents containing this type of information were created with the express intention of sharing that information. Consider the screen shown in Figure 11.53, which was submitted by CP.

SUMMARY

This chapter is all about what can go drastically wrong when the Google hacking threat is ignored. Use this chapter whenever you have trouble conveying the seriousness of the threat. Help spread the word, and become part of the solution and not part of the problem. And before you go sending cease and desist papers to Google, remember – it's not Google's fault if your sensitive data makes it online.

CHAPTER 12

Protecting Yourself from Google Hackers

INTRODUCTION

The purpose of this book is to help you understand the tactics a Google hacker might employ so that you can properly protect yourself and your customers from this seemingly innocuous threat. The best way to do this, in my opinion, is to show you exactly what an attacker armed with a search engine like Google is capable of. There is a point at which we must discuss in no uncertain terms *exactly* how to prevent this type of information exposure or how to remedy an existing exposure. This chapter is all about protecting your site (or your customer's site) from this type of attack.

We'll look at this topic from several perspectives. First, it's important that you understand the value of strong policy with regard to posting data on the Internet. This is not a technical topic and could very easily put the techie in you fast asleep, but a sound security policy is absolutely necessary when it comes to properly securing any site. Second, we'll look at slightly more technical topics that describe how to secure your Web site from Google's (and other search engine's) crawlers. We'll then look at some tools that can be used to help check a Web site's Google exposure, and we'll spend some time talking about ways Google can help you shore up your defenses.

There are too many types of servers and configurations to show how to lock them all down. A discussion on Web server security could easily span an entire book series. We'll look at server security at a high level here, focusing on strategies you can employ to specifically protect you from the Google hacker threat. For more details, please check the references in the Section "Links to Sites."

A GOOD SOLID SECURITY POLICY

The best hardware and software configuration that money can buy can't protect your resources if you don't have an effective security policy. Before implementing any software assurances, take the time to review your security policy.

A good security policy, properly enforced, outlines the assets you're trying to protect, how the protection mechanisms are installed, the acceptable level of operational risk, and what to do in the event of a compromise or disaster. Without a solid, enforced security policy, you're fighting a losing battle.

WEB SERVER SAFEGUARDS

There are several ways to keep the prying eyes of a Web crawler from digging too deeply into your site. However, bear in mind that a Web server is designed to store data that is meant for public consumption. Despite all the best protections, information leaks happen. If you're really concerned about keeping your sensitive information private, keep it away from your public Web server. Move that data to an intranet or onto a specialized server that is dedicated to serving that information in a safe, responsible, policy-enforced manner.

Don't get in the habit of splitting a public Web server into distinct roles based on access levels. It's too easy for a user to copy data from one file to another, which could render some directory-based protection mechanisms useless. Likewise, consider the implications of a public Web server system compromise. In a well-thoughtout, properly constructed environment, the compromise of a public Web server only results in the compromise of public information. Proper access restrictions would prevent the attacker from bouncing from the Web server to any other machine, making further infiltration of more sensitive information all the more difficult for the attacker. If sensitive information were stored alongside public information on a public Web server, the compromise of that server could potentially compromise the more sensitive information as well.

We'll begin by taking a look at some fairly simple measures that can be taken to lock down a Web server from within. These are general principles; they're not meant to provide a complete solution but rather to highlight some of the common key areas of defense. We will not focus on any specific type of server but will look at suggestions that should be universal to any Web server. We will not delve into the specifics of protecting a Web *application*, but rather we'll explore more common methods that have proven especially and specifically effective against Web crawlers.

Directory Listings and Missing Index Files

We've already seen the risks associated with directory listings. Although minor information leaks, directory listings allow the Web user to see most (if not all) of the files in a directory, as well as any lower-level subdirectories. As opposed to the "guided" experience of surfing through a series of prepared pages, directory listings provide much more unfettered access. Depending on many factors, such as the permissions of the files and directories as well as the server's settings for allowed files, even a casual Web browser could get access to files that should not be public.

Normally, this file (which should be called *.htaccess*, not *htaccess*) serves to protect the directory contents from unauthorized viewing. However, a server misconfiguration allows this file to be seen in a directory listing and even read.

Directory listings should be disabled unless you intend to allow visitors to peruse files in an FTP-style. On some servers, a directory listing will appear if an index file (as defined by your server configuration) is missing. These files, such as index.html, index.htm, or default.asp, should appear in each and every directory that should present a page to the user. On an Apache Web server, you can disable directory listings by placing a dash or minus sign before the word *Indexes* in the httpd.conf file. The line might look something like this if directory listings (or "indexes," as Apache calls them) are disabled:

```
Options -Indexes FollowSymLinksMultiViews
```

Robots.txt: Preventing Caching

The robots.txt file provides a list of instructions for automated Web crawlers, also called *robots* or *bots*. Standardized at www.robotstxt.org/wc/norobots.html, this file allows you to define, with a great deal of precision, which files and directories are off-limits to Web robots. The robots.txt file must be placed in the root of the Web server with permissions that allow the Web server to read the file. Lines in the file beginning with a # sign are considered comments and are ignored. Each line not beginning with a # should begin with either a *User-agent* or a *disallow* statement, followed by a colon and an optional space. These lines are written to disallow certain crawlers from accessing certain directories or files. Each Web crawler should send a *user-agent* field, which lists the name or type of the crawler. The value of Google's *user-agent* field is *Googlebot*. To address a *disallow* to Google, the *user-agent* line should read:

```
User-agent: Googlebot
```

According to the original specification, the wildcard character * can be used in the *user-agent* field to indicate all crawlers. The *disallow* line describes what, exactly; the crawler should *not* look at. The original specifications for this file were fairly inflexible, stating that a disallow line could only address a full or partial URL. According to that original specification, the crawler would ignore any URL *starting with* the specified string. For example, a line like *Disallow: /foo* would instruct the crawler to ignore not only */foo* but */foo/index.html*, whereas a line like *Disallow: /foo/* would instruct the crawler to ignore */foo/index.html* but *not /foo*, since the slash trailing *foo* must exist. For example, a valid robots.txt file is shown here:

#abandon hope all ye who enter User-Agent: *Disallow: /

This file indicates that no crawler is allowed on any part of the site – the ultimate exclude for Web crawlers. The robots.txt file is read from top to bottom as ordered rules. There is no *allow* line in a robots.txt file. To include a particular crawler, disallow its access to *nothing*. This might seem like backward logic, but the following robots.txt file indicates that all crawlers are to be sent away *except* for the crawler named *Palookaville*:

#Bring on Palookaville User-Agent: *Disallow: / User-Agent: Palookaville Disallow:

Notice that there is no slash after Palookaville's *disallow*. (Norman Cook fans will be delighted to notice the absence of both slashes *and* dots from anywhere near Palookaville.) Saying that there's no *disallow* is like saying that user agent is *allowed* – sloppy and confusing, but that's the way it is.

Google allows for extensions to the robots.txt standard. A disallow pattern may include * to match any number of characters. In addition, a $ indicates the end of a name. For example, to prevent the Googlebot from crawling all your PDF documents, you can use the following robots.txt file:

#Away from my PDF files, Google! User-Agent: Googlebot Disallow: /*.PDF$

Once you've gotten a robots.txt file in place, you can check its validity by visiting the Robots.txt Validator at www.sxw.org.uk/computing/robots/check.html.

Hackers don't have to obey your robots.txt file. In fact, Web crawlers really don't have to either, although most of the big-name Web crawlers will, if only for the "CYA" factor. One fairly common hacker trick is to view a site's robots.txt file first to get an idea of how files and directories are mapped on the server. In fact a quick Google query can reveal lots of sites that have had their robots.txt files *crawled*. This, of course, is a misconfiguration, because the robots.txt file is meant to stay behind the scenes.

NOARCHIVE: The Cache "Killer"

The robots.txt file keeps Google away from certain areas of your site. However, there could be cases where you want Google to crawl a page, but you don't want Google to cache a copy of the page or present a "cached" link in its search results. This is accomplished with a *META* tag. To prevent all (cooperating) crawlers from archiving or caching a document, place the following *META* tag in the *HEAD* section of the document:

```
<META NAME="ROBOTS" CONTENT="NOARCHIVE">
```

If you prefer to keep *only* Google from caching the document, use this *META* tag in the *HEAD* section of the document:

```
<META NAME="GOOGLEBOT" CONTENT="NOINDEX, NOFOLLOW">
```

Any cooperating crawler can be addressed in this way by inserting its name as the *META NAME*. Understand that this rule only addresses crawlers. Web visitors (and hackers) can still access these pages.

NOSNIPPET: Getting Rid of Snippets

A *snippet* is the text listed below the title of a document on the Google results page. Providing insight into the returned document, snippets are convenient when you're blowing through piles of results. However, in some cases, snippets should be removed. Consider the case of a subscription-based news service. Although this type of site would like to have the kind of exposure that Google can offer, it needs to protect its content (including snippets of content) from nonpaying subscribers. Such a site can accomplish this goal by combining the *NOSNIPPET META* tag with IP-based filters that allow Google's crawlers to browse content unmolested. To keep Google from displaying snippets, insert this code into the document:

```
<META NAME="GOOGLEBOT" CONTENT="NOSNIPPET">
```

An interesting side effect of the *NOSNIPPET* tag is that Google will not cache the document. *NOSNIPPET* removes both the snippet and the cached page.

Password-Protected Mechanisms

Google does not fill in user authentication forms. When presented with a typical password form, Google seems to simply back away from that page, keeping nothing but the page's URL in its database. Although it was once rumored that Google bypasses or somehow magically side-steps security checks, those rumors have never been substantiated. These incidents are more likely an issue of timing.

If Google crawls a password-protected page either before the page is protected or while the password protection is down, Google will cache an image of the protected page. Clicking the original page will show the password dialog, but the cached page does not – providing the illusion that Google has bypassed that page's security. In other cases, a Google news search will provide a snippet of a news story from a subscription site, but clicking the link to the story presents a registration screen. This also creates the illusion that Google somehow magically bypasses pesky password dialogs and registration screens.

If you're really serious about keeping the general public (and crawlers like Google) away from your data, consider a password authentication mechanism. A basic password authentication mechanism, htaccess, exists for Apache. An htaccess file, combined with an htpasswd file, allows you to define a list of username/password combinations that can access specific directories. You'll find an Apache htaccess tutorial at http://httpd.apache.org/docs/howto/htac-cess.html, or try a Google search for *htaccess howto*.

SOFTWARE DEFAULT SETTINGS AND PROGRAMS

As we've seen throughout this book, even the most basic Google hacker can home in on default pages, phrases, page titles, programs, and documentation with very little effort. Keep this in mind and remove these items from any Web software you install. It's also good security practice to ensure that default accounts and passwords are removed as well as any installation scripts or programs that were supplied with the software. Since the topic of Web server security is so vast, we'll take a look at some of the highlights you should consider for a few common servers.

It certainly sounds like a cliché in today's security circles, but it can't be stressed enough: If you choose to do only one thing to secure any of your systems, it should be to keep up with and install all the latest software security patches. Misconfigurations make for a close second, but without a firm foundation, your server doesn't stand a chance.

HACKING YOUR OWN SITE

Hacking into your own site is a great way to get an idea of its potential security risks. Obviously, no single person can know everything there is to know about hacking, meaning that hacking your own site is no replacement for having a real penetration test performed by a professional. Even if you are a pen tester by trade, it never hurts to have another perspective on your security posture. In the realm of Google hacking, there are several automated tools and techniques you can use to give yourself another perspective on how Google sees your site. We'll start by looking at some manual methods, and we'll finish by discussing some automated alternatives.

As we'll see in this chapter, there are several ways a Google search can be automated. Google frowns on any method that does not use its supplied Application Programming Interface (API) along with a Google license key. Assume that any program that does not ask you for your license key is running in violation of Google's terms of service and could result in banishment from Google. Check out www.google.com/accounts/TOS for more information. Be nice to Google and Google will be nice to you!

Site Yourself

We've talked about the *site* operator throughout the book, but remember that *site* allows you to narrow a search to a particular domain or server. If you're Sullo, the author of the (most impressive) NIKTO tool and administrator of cirt.net, a query like *site:cirt.net* will list all Google's cached pages from your cirt.net server.

You could certainly click each and every one of these links or simply browse through the list of results to determine if those pages are indeed supposed to be public, but this exercise could be very time consuming, especially if the number of results is more than a few hundred.

WIKTO

Wikto is an amazing Web scanning tool written by Roloef Temmingh while he was with Sensepost (www.sensepost.com). Wikto does many different things, but since this book focuses on Google hacking, we'll take a look at the Google scanning portions of the tool. By default, Wikto launches a wizard interface. Wikto will first prompt for the target you wish to scan, as well as details about the target server. Clicking the *Next* button loads the *Configuration* panel. This panel prompts for proxy information and asks for your Google API key. The API issue is tricky, as Google is no longer giving out SOAP API keys. If you already have a SOAP API key, lucky you.

Notice that the output fields list files and directories that were located on the target site. All of this information was gathered through Google queries, meaning the transactions are transparent to the target. Wikto will use this directory and file information in later scanning stages.

Next, we'll take a look at the *GoogleHacks* tab.

This scanning phase relies on the Google Hacking Database. Clicking the *Load Google Hacks Database* will load the most current version of the GHDB, providing Wikto with thousands of potentially malicious Google queries. Once the GHDB is loaded, pressing the *Start* button will begin the Google scan of the target site. What's basically happening here is Wikto is firing off tons of Google queries, each with a *site* operator which points to the target Web site. The GHDB is shown in the upper panel, and any results are presented in the lower panel. Clicking on a result in the lower panel will show the detailed information about that query (from the GHDB) in the middle panel.

In addition to this automated scanning process, Wikto allows you to perform manual Google queries against the target through the use of the *Manual Query* button and the associated input field.

Wikto is an amazing tool with loads of features. Combined with GHDB compatibility, Wikto is definitely the best Google hacking tool currently available.

ADVANCE DORK

Advanced Dork is an extension for Firefox and Mozilla browsers, which provides Google Advanced Operators for use directly from the right-click context menu. Written by CP, the tool is available from https://addons.mozilla.org/en-US/firefox/addon/2144.

Like all Firefox extensions, installation is a snap: simply click the link to the .xpi file from within Firefox and the installation will launch.

Advanced Dork is context sensitive – right-clicking will invoke Advanced Dork based on where the right-click was performed. For example, right-clicking on a link will invoke link-specific options.

Right-clicking on a highlighted text will invoke the highlighted text search mode of Advanced Dork

This mode will allow you to use the highlighted word in an *intitle, inurl, intext, site* or *ext* search. Several awesome options are available to Advanced Dork.

Advanced Dork is an amazing tool for any serious Google user. You should definitely add it to your arsenal.

GETTING HELP FROM GOOGLE

So far we've looked at various ways of checking your site for potential information leaks, but what can you do if you detect such leaks? First and foremost, you should remove the offending content from your site. This may be a fairly involved process, but to do it right, you should always figure out the source of the leak, to ensure that similar leaks don't happen in the future. Information leaks don't just happen; they are the result of some event that occurred. Figure out the event, resolve it, and you can begin to stem the source of the problem. Solving the local problem is only half the battle. In some cases, Google has a cached copy of your information leak just waiting to be picked up by a Google hacker.

SUMMARY

The subject of Web server security is too big for any one book. There are so many varied requirements combined with so many different types of Web server software, application software, and operating system software that not a single book could do justice to the topic. However, a few general principles can at least help you prevent the devastating effects a malicious Google hacker could inflict on a site you're charged with protecting.

First, understand how the Web server software operates in the event of an unexpected condition. Directory listings, missing index files, and specific error messages can all open up avenues for offensive information gathering. Robots.txt files, simple password authentication, and effective use of *META* tags can help steer Web crawlers away from specific areas of your site. Although Web data is generally considered public, remember that Google hackers might take interest in your site if it appears as a result of a malicious Google search. Default pages, directories and programs can serve as an indicator that there is a low level of technical know-how behind a site. Servers with this type of default information serve as targets for hackers. Get a handle on what, exactly; a search engine needs to know about your site to draw visitors without attracting undue attention as a result of too much exposure. Use any of the available tools, such as Gooscan, Wikto, Advanced Dork, to help you search Google for your site's information leaks. If you locate a page that shouldn't be public, use Google's removal tools to flush the page from Google's database.

FAST TRACK SOLUTIONS

A Good, Solid Security Policy

- An enforceable, solid security policy should serve as the foundation of any security effort.
- Without a policy, your safeguards could be inefficient or unenforceable.

Web Server Safeguards

- Directory listings, error messages, and misconfigurations can provide too much information.
- Robots.txt files and specialized *META* tags can help direct search engine crawlers away from specific pages or directories.

- Password mechanisms, even basic ones, keep crawlers away from protected content.
- Default pages and settings indicate that a server is not well maintained and can make that server a target.

Hacking Your Own Site

- Use the *site* operator to browse the servers you're charged with protecting. Keep an eye out for any pages that don't belong there.
- Use a tool like Gooscan, or Advanced Dork to assess your exposure. These tools do not use the Google API, so be aware that any blatant abuse or excessive activity could get your IP range cut off from Google.
- Use a tool like Wikto, which uses the Google API and should free you from fear of getting shut down.
- Use the Google Hacking Database to monitor the latest Google hacking queries. Use the GHDB exports with tools like Gooscan, or Wikto.

Getting Help from Google

- Use Google's Webmaster page for information specifically geared toward Webmasters.
- Use Google's URL removal tools to get sensitive data out of Google's databases.

LINKS TO SITES

- **http://www.exploit-db.com/google-dorks/** – The home of the Google Hacking Database (GHDB), the search engine hacking forums, the Gooscan tool, and the GHDB export files.
- **http://www.seorank.com/robots-tutorial.htm** – A good tutorial on using the robots.txt file.
  - http://googleblog.blogspot.com/2007/02/robots-exclusion-protocol.html – Information about Google's Robots policy.
- **https://addons.mozilla.org/en-US/firefox/addon/2144** – Home of Cp's Advanced Dork

Subject Index

Printed in the United States
By Bookmasters